Helion & Company Limited
Unit 8 Amherst Business Centre
Budbrooke Road
Warwick
CV34 5WE
England
Tel. 01926 499 619
Email: info@helion.co.uk
Website: www.helion.co.uk
Twitter: @helionbooks
https://helionbooks.wordpress.com/

Artworks: Luca Canossa, Tom Cooper, Renato Dalmasso & Goran Sudar
Maps: Tom Cooper

Cover image: During the autumn of 1991, pilots from the 249th Fighter-Bomber Aviation Squadron operating from Udbina Air Base in the central Lika region of Croatia were deployed for combat missions. Before the war this unit was originally tasked with training pilot students from the Air Force Academy. The Galeb-4 aircraft used by this squadron were mainly new, produced between 1989 and 1990, and were received directly from the Soko factory in Mostar. Therefore, during the war, the standard camouflage scheme of the Air Force and Air Defence had a 'fresh' appearance. They also carried a small unit emblem of the 249th Squadron in the form of a cobra. (Milorad Ristić).

Designed and typeset by Mach 3 Solutions (www.mach3solutions.co.uk)
Cover design Paul Hewitt, Battlefield Design (www.battlefield-design.co.uk)

ISBN: 978-1-914059-17-9

British Library Cataloguing-in-Publication Data
A catalogue record for this book is available from the British Library

We always welcome receiving book proposals from prospective authors.

CONTENTS

EDITORIAL NOTE

All military ranks are as in official use at the time of the described events. Unless stated otherwise, all times are local times. While only the first letter of official designations of institutions and services of the Yugoslav armed forces was written in capital letters, and this practice was subsequently adopted in Croatia and Slovenia, their translations in this book are written as per Standard English. When mentioned for the first time in the text, aircraft and heavy weapons system designations are cited fully – including their designer and/or the manufacturer, official military designation and nickname: in the case of Soviet-made armament: this is followed by the ASCC/NATO codename, but through the text only their original designations are used. Local, Yugoslav designations are provided in separate tables. Unless cited in the endnotes, all sources are interviews with participants or original documentation listed in the bibliography. For easier understanding of ranks of the Yugoslav Air Force used in this book, an appendix is included comparing these with ranks in the US Air Force and the Royal Air Force (United Kingdom) from the highest non-commissioned officer rank, to the highest officer rank.

ABBREVIATIONS AND ACRONYMNS

AA	anti-aircraft
AB	air base
APC	armoured personnel carrier
ATGM	anti-tank guided missile
CAS	close air support
ECMM	European Community Monitor Mission
ELINT	electronic intelligence
HEAT	high-explosive anti-tank
HQ	Headquarters
IFV	infantry fighting vehicle
JNA	*Jugoslovenska narodna armija* (Yugoslav armed forces – all branches/in general – and colloquial for the Yugoslav army/ground forces, 1952–1991)
LOROP	Long Range Oblique Photography
MANPADS	man-portable air defence system
MBT	main battle tank
MD	Military District (*Vojna oblast* in the JNA)
NATO	North Atlantic Treaty Organization
NCO	non-commissioned officer
OG	*Operativna grupa* (Task Force)
QRA	Quick Reaction Alert
POW	prisoner of war
RV i PVO	*Ratno vazduhoplovstvo i protivvazdušna odbrana* (Yugoslav Air Force and Air Defence Force, used 1959–1991)
SAM	surface-to-air missile
SFRJ	*Socijalistička Federativna Republika Jugoslavija* (Socialist Federal Republic of Yugoslavia)
ŠVK	*Štab Vrhovne komande* (High command, JNA, established in January 1991)
TO	*Teritorijalna odbrana* (Territorial Defence)
USA	United States of America
USAF	United States Air Force
VMA	*Vojnomedicinska akademija* (Military Medical Academy)
VVA	*Vazduhoplovna vojna akademija* (Air Force Academy of the RV i PVO)
ZNG	*Zbor narodne garde* (Croat National Guard, 1991–1994)

INTRODUCTION

In Volume 1, I attempted to depict the complexity of the Yugoslav crisis and the circumstances that gradually led the apparently harmonious multinational state into a bloody civil war. In Kosovo in 1981, ethnic Albanians initiated massive demonstrations and actions against the then-Militia (*Milicija*, Police) and the first casualties occurred on both sides. Due to a new wave of riots in 1989 in Kosovo, the Yugoslav National Army (*Jugoslovenska narodna armija*, JNA) and Militia intervened. Political leaders in Slovenia and Croatia, relying on a significant portion of support from public opinion, were preparing to exit the Yugoslav federation. In Beograd (Belgrade), the stance of the JNA's leadership was to preserve the Socialist Federal Republic of Yugoslavia (*Socijalisticka Federativna Republika Jugoslavija*, SFRJ), or at least a portion of the territory that wanted to live together. Serbs in Croatia were antagonistic towards the Croatian leadership, and on 17 August 1990, their armed militia – based on the local structure of the Territorial Defence (*Teritorijalna odbrana*, TO) erected barricades on the roads in the interior of northern *Dalmacija* (Dalmatia). This date, from the Serbian point of view, is considered the beginning of the crisis, and participation in the war for those in uniform is counted from that day. According to Croatian regulations, the status of a participant in the armed forces is calculated from 5 August 1990.

These were administrative measures, but the months following the first incidents were reduced to tensions and preparations for war without major conflict. Croatians formed their national armed forces under the legal framework of the Ministry of the Interior. Serbs in Croatia unilaterally established the Autonomous Region of Krajina, whose uniformed members bore the insignia of their militia.

The first two casualties, ironically one Croat and one Serb, resulted from the conflict on 31 March 1991, in the Plitvice Lakes National Park, an idyllic cascade of lakes and waterfalls within a dense forest in the Lika region. Federal authorities sent a JNA task force with the assignment of separating forces in the conflict. In the shadow of this major rift between Serbs and Croats, a short drama unfolded in

Slovenia from 26 June to 3 July 1991. The political decision for the JNA to withdraw from Slovenia marked the end of the SFRJ.

During the summer of 1991, occasional incidents in Croatia gradually escalated into open armed conflict in which military and civilian casualties continuously grew. On one side were the nascent Croatian armed forces, initially a heterogeneous mix of police and paramilitary forces formed under the legal umbrella of the Ministry of Internal Affairs and Civil Defence, and the remnants of the TO from the Yugoslav defence system. On the other side were Serbs in Croatia, organised partly as the police, partly in paramilitary units, some under the control of Beograd through the State Security (*državna bezbednost*) responsible for covert operations. In the deeply ideological era of communism, the JNA was not inclined toward nationalism, and therefore, it attempted to control the armed formations on the ground in Krajina.

Initially, the Federal armed forces attempted to maintain a neutral stance between the two sides, but gradually, they began intervening in the war. First with the task of lifting the blockade of its garrisons surrounded by Croatian forces and then with the task of gaining control, and securing the territory of the self-declared Krajina, predominantly populated by the Serbs.

During the fighting in Croatia in the summer and autumn of 1991, preparations for a mutual confrontation began in Bosnia and Herzegovina among the three major ethnic communities: Muslims, Serbs, and Croats. The official rhetoric of politicians was full of general phrases about maintaining peace, but mobilisation lists of battalions for the future war were secretly compiled. The first international body to be drawn into the war was the European Community, which deployed its European Community Monitor Mission (ECMM), recognisable by white uniforms and restrained attitude. Due to their appearance and actions, they were referred to as benign 'ice cream sellers' who observed what was happening and did not have authorisation for concrete measures. As the Yugoslav

One MiG-29 pilot in the 127th Fighter Aviation Squadron in 1991 was Milenko Pavlovic, who had the credentials of one of the best fighter pilots in Yugoslavia. He rose rapidly in his career in the 1990s and at the time of the NATO air attacks in 1999 he was the commander of the 204th Fighter Aviation Regiment. He lost his life on 4 May 1999 in a MiG-29 that was hit by AMRAAM missiles fired from a USAF F-16. (Dragan Veličković)

One of the last pre-war photographs of an RV i PVO aircraft was taken in May 1991 when pilot Dragan Veličković, at that time a journalist for the military magazine *Front*, flew with colleagues from the 351st Reconnaissance Aviation Squadron based at Cerklje. Above Slovenia, a series of photographs were taken of this IJ-22 Orao with reconnaissance pod. When the fighting began in the north-west Federal unit of the SFRJ in June 1991, all aircraft were withdrawn, and number 25710 was handed over to the 353rd Squadron at Mostar Air Base. It changed bases again in May 1992 when, under pressure from the war in Herzegovina, the unit transferred to Lađevci Air Base in central Serbia. According to the Sub-Regional Arms Control Agreement of 1996, a portion of the combat aircraft was withdrawn from service, including one numbered 25710. It was placed as a monument in the town of Topola next to a plaque with the names of those who died in the civil war from 1991 to 1995. One of them was Zoran Tomić, a pilot who died on a combat mission in a J-22 Orao on 17 September 1991. (Dragan Veličković)

In autumn 1991, regular ceremonies and parades were held in the RV i PVO in honour of the Yugoslav-era holidays. This photograph shows members of the 138th Brigade lined up at the base in Batajnica, about 100km from the front. Officers and pilots are in standard pre-war service uniforms and blue pilot overalls. Combat aircraft pilots had priority in switching to camouflage suits. (Vilijam Horvat)

RV i PVO flight suits carried just the official branch insignia on the left sleeve and the rank on the right side of the chest. During the war months, some pilots wore SFRJ flags as a symbol of their attitude that the Federal state was being defended. (Author's collection)

During the summer and autumn of 1991 MiG-29s at Batajnica base stood Quick Reaction Alert (QRA) armed with two R-27R1 semi-active radar-homing air-to-air missiles and four R-60MK short-range infrared air-to- air missiles. (Dragan Veličković)

crisis continued into the 1990s, NATO's influence became crucial; however, at the beginning of the Yugoslav War, it was an internal conflict that started and played out on the periphery of the attention of the Western powers, which were focussed on the fall of the Eastern Bloc.

Overall, the aim of this volume is to present the course of events during the autumn of 1991, primarily in Croatia, and through the period of mid-September until mid-November. During this period, the Croatian forces blockaded JNA bases until an agreement was reached and signed in Geneva, Switzerland, about a temporary cessation of hostilities, lifting the blockades, and the withdrawal of the JNA from Croatia. The document was signed by individuals who had effective power in shaping the situation on the ground; Army General Veljko Kadijević (Federal Secretary for National Defence), Slobodan Milošević (President of Serbia), and Franjo Tuđman (President of Croatia).

1
OPERATION KRILO

The decisive date in the relationship between Croatia and the JNA was 13 September 1991, when an order from the Croatian leadership was issued to implement a complete active blockade of all barracks and warehouses and to occupy them if the opportunity presented itself, by force if necessary. At that time, the activities were coordinated by the Main Staff of the Army of Croatia (*Glavni stožer Hrvatske vojske*, GSHV), which was led by the previous CO of the Croatian Armed Forces and air defence forces (PVO), and former General of the RV i PVO: Colonel General Anton Tus. In his post-war statements, he said that Croatian President Franjo Tuđman approved the actions, but also determined them to remain of limited effect: 'Good, but don't immediately attack the barracks and warehouses in Zagreb, Rijeka and Istria so that we have a partially peaceful territory'.[1]

Tus might not have ordered a simultaneous attack on all the bases. Nevertheless, in the first few weeks of the blockade, Croatian forces obtained huge quantities of weapons which provided the material resources for their buildup into dozens of brigades.

Strategic Position of the JNA and the RV i PVO as of September 1991

The negotiations in Geneva, mediated by the representatives of the European Community (EC), Lord Peter Carrington, and the United Nations (UN), Cyrus Vance, did not completely halt the fighting in Croatia during 1991, but they did enable the JNA to withdraw the forces and equipment of several major garrisons, primarily those in the area of the Croat capital, Zagreb. By that time, many officers and other ranks of both the JNA and the RV i PVO had left active service or deserted. This process began with the decision of the JNA to withdraw from Slovenia in the summer of 1991, when all Slovenians were offered the opportunity to leave the RV i PVO. Very few chose to remain and the departure of a significant number of ethnic Slovenians during the summer of 1991 – most of them having left according to the regular procedure, at their own request – along with the departure of Croats, affected the staffing of the RV i PVO units.[2]

Whether based in the two western republics, in Bosnia, in Serbia, in Montenegro, or Macedonia, officers and other ranks of all nationalities were subjected to strong war propaganda and even direct pressure. Consequently, some units retained strong cohesion, but some were left without a significant portion of their officers in the first wave of departures from the JNA. Those deployed in Slovenia and Croatia were hit particularly hard; those home-based in Bosnia and Herzegovina, Serbia, Macedonia, and Montenegro largely retained their multi-ethnic composition. An exception was the 252nd Fighter-Bomber Aviation Squadron, whose pilots were of almost exclusively Serbian ethnicity. As a result, one reinforced squadron and one flight were formed from the 82nd Aviation Brigade, which previously had three squadrons. That said, the branch command was led by generals and officers of Yugoslav provenance, the mass of whom demonstrated indifference to nationalism.

On the ground, the majority of units that found themselves under blockade in Croatia were critically short of personnel, and did not have the capability to organise a breakout. Their activities involved passive defence with anti-personnel mines and demonstration actions against surrounding infrastructure. When the fighting intensified, some units targeted facilities used by the Croatian armed forces, with tanks, anti-aircraft guns, mortars, anti-tank guns and machine guns. In some cases, their commanders even ordered firing upon civilian facilities, or those with dual purposes. Beograd was most concerned for those serving in the garrisons in the western part of the SFRJ: the uncertainty about the fate of families that had not evacuated from cities in Slovenia and Croatia had a significant impact on morale. The situation worsened during the summer of 1991, as heightened combat readiness resulted in officers and other ranks effectively being locked into their bases, while their families were in nearby civilian settlements. Moreover, while unable to capture large, well-defended and well-armed bases, the Croats were able to blockade them from the outside world: as the nascent Croatian armed forces began severing telephone lines, it became extremely difficult to verify the situation of dependants.

Some officers managed to move their families to the safety of bases; some even managed to bring a number of ethnic Serbs there. However, many others did not. The situation was neither straightforward, nor the same in any two different places, even more so as periods of intense confrontation and complete blockade alternated with de-escalation periods agreed at the local level between Croatian crisis headquarters (HQ) and JNA commanders. The situation was one where shots might be fired at any movement within the barracks, and then the delivery of food and water was allowed.

The resulting stalemate was resolved through the above-mentioned negotiations, and agreements on the evacuation of units with weapons, implemented in the period from November to December 1991. The painful war that was to follow caused many personal tragedies and personal stories, often tearing families apart due to national divisions.

Confusion in Beograd

A particularly important aspect of the atmosphere in the war-torn Yugoslavia during the autumn of 1991 was the confusion about the goals of the JNA. The Federal government all but disappeared. The average JNA member – or an airman of the RV i PVO – did not understand what needed to be achieved on the battlefield. Internal information inherited from the communist era imposed a one-sided stance that the war was fought to preserve Yugoslavia, but the real conditions on the ground pointed to political agreements, as seen in the case of Slovenia: in just a few days in July 1991, the JNA went from intending to launch massive air attacks to the order to leave that part of the SFRJ.

At the top of the armed forces was the Supreme Command Staff (*Štab Vrhovne Komande*, ŠVK), which functioned as a separate holder of political power in the SFRJ, with significant influence from several leading generals who were communist hardliners. Ideological and rigid bureaucratic mechanisms of thinking by senior officers resulted in them being caught by surprise by developments: they failed to react to new circumstances and rapid changes and the collapse of the Federal model. An example of the discourse of that time in the JNA, is the following quote from the part of the analysis of combat readiness of the Air Force Academy (*Vazduhoplovna vojna akademija*, VAA) in 1991:

> The basic characteristics of the movement in the international community are manifested through the historical change in the balance of power in the world, which is characterised by the collapse of the Warsaw Pact and the disappearance of real socialism. Developed capitalist countries create a completely free space for the realisation of their goals. The influence of non-aligned countries is objectively disappearing from the international scene. The expansion of Germany gives the basic characteristic of relations in Europe. It has a specially developed interest towards Yugoslavia, i.e. its parts. The polarising political forces in Yugoslavia had the comprehensive support of the international factor in achieving its nationalist interests and the breakup of Yugoslavia, which led to armed conflicts.[3]

Hard ideological explanations were not the answer to what the JNA needed, and that is why the analysis of the VVA states that officers asked questions like, 'Are Yugoslavia and the JNA at war and if so, what are the strategic goals of that war?'

The goals defined by the ŠVK had no force and no value upon which the unity and fighting morale of all members of the VVA, and thus the RV i PVO, could be built, especially considering the mixed national composition of the service (just like the entire JNA). The absence of a clear perspective of Yugoslavia and the JNA as its institution led to the constant questioning of some members, whether they were on the 'right' side and whether they should remain in the JNA.

On the other hand: on the part of the secessionists in Slovenia and Croatia, for example, the definition of the war goals was very simple: to get rid of the SFRJ and the JNA, to declare and establish their own sovereign states. The Slovenians achieved this in the short war described in Volume 1 of this work. On 7 July 1991, the Croats, like the Slovenians, accepted the Brioni Declaration (or Agreement) on the three-month frozen status. The differences were big because the JNA had withdrawn from Slovenia, but was now in the process of being introduced to the fighting in Croatia.

The fighting between the Federal and Croatian armed forces was an important security subject in the world in 1991. American Defence and Air Attache Colonel Gene Whisnant was informed by the CO RV i PVO Major General Zvonko Jurjević about the situation at the front. The American officer understood the war environment because he was a USAF combat cameraman in Vietnam and flew on 32 missions. (Vilijam Horvat)

Seen here on the underwing pylon of a Galeb-2 from the 252nd Squadron is a 5-inch HVAR Mk 25 rocket with a HEAT warhead. At the beginning of the war, there were considerable quantities of these stored in the warehouses of the RV i PVO, inherited from the American Military Assistance Program from the 1950s. Their stocks were used up during the fighting in 1991–1992. (Dragan Veličković)

The blockaded barracks were under constant attack by the Croatian armed forces and this photograph shows the effects upon the Air Force Training Centre building in Zadar. Metal boxes and books were placed in the windows to protect the soldiers. (Branislav Rumenić)

A Zastava 101 military passenger car, destroyed in the grounds of Ante Banina barracks in Zadar. Visible behind it is a BOV-3 self-propelled anti-aircraft gun used to defend the barracks. (Branislav Rumenić)

Blockade of Military Bases

Many units of the JNA surrendered quickly because they lacked the personnel and motivation for combat. Indeed, in addition to the lack of clear task and purpose at the strategic level, the biggest shortcoming of the JNA was the weak staffing of units with personnel at the time when the Croats blockaded the barracks. The pre-war model of total defence envisaged three classification ranks for units:

- 'A' which in peacetime had 60–100 percent of the personnel envisioned for full wartime composition
- 'B' with 15–60 percent of the cadre, and
- 'R' with up to 15 percent, or rather only the command cadre, but suitable for wartime expansion.

Equipment and other materials for lower-level units were kept in barracks and warehouses. During the summer of 1991, the JNA saw a decreasing number of recruits, and the actual number of people in units became almost symbolic. Therefore, when considering the order of battle for the Federal forces as of 1991, it should be kept in mind that this represents nominal unit designations, but that the majority of the assets in question existed on paper only. This problem was particularly true for the ground forces. On the other hand, nearly all of the units of the RV i PVO were classified as 'A': even if not having 100 percent of their required personnel, most of them held up against all external pressures.

Aircraft of the RV i PVO were used in the protection of JNA barracks, but very rarely in direct action against Croatian units. The situation on the ground was often unclear, and the distances between friendly and enemy forces too small for effective close air support (CAS) without the risk of inflicting friendly fire casualties. Therefore, action was taken against Croatian positions only where the line was known, and occasionally against infrastructure that the Croats had taken.

Land forces often requested air strikes on inappropriate and mobile targets. One MiG-21bis pilot recalled the frustrations he had when tasked with flying with a colleague on a cloudy autumn day to locate and destroy a mortar on a wooded hill. In practice, this was an unachievable task with high risk.

The cost of the confusion in the initial phase of the open conflict for the RV i PVO was high: out of 25 of its aircraft destroyed over Croatia, no fewer than nine were shot down in just five days between 16 and 20 September 1991. During this period, one aircraft and pilot went missing on a combat mission and was probably shot down. The RV i PVO lost six people (five pilots and one technical officer), and two pilots became prisoners of war.

The series of shootdowns and damage to aircraft confronted RV i PVO pilots with the harsh reality of war. Strela-2M missiles proved to be particularly effective, but at that time no aircraft in the RV i PVO, except the MiG-29, had infrared flares. The tactics for attacks had to be quickly adapted, but military bureaucracy was satisfied with routine analyses of shootdowns, demanding special tactical preparation and security for each combat flight, actions to be executed in one sortie with minimal dwell time above targets. It was proposed to develop tactical procedures for actions from higher altitudes and extremely low altitudes outside established patterns for rocketing and bombing, using manoeuvres against anti-aircraft (AA) guns and man-portable air defence systems (MANPADS) on approach and departure. Three aircraft were shot down and eight were damaged from the 252nd Squadron, and the pilots agreed to switch to releasing combat loads at an altitude of 2,000–2,500 m.

A particular problem was the risk of loss during repeated passes as some aircraft were shot down on the third attack on the same target. Therefore, in some units, such as the 117th Aviation Brigade, they decided to arm MiG-21s with only two pylons, and only one sortie was executed in the target area.

ALOUETTE III

The Brioni Declaration, signed on 7 July between official representatives of Belgrade and representatives of Slovenia and Croatia, under the supervision of the EC, served as the legal basis for the first international military mission in the territory of the SFRJ. Officers and non-commissioned officers (NCOs) from EC member states arrived on the ground to observe the situation. Their headquarters was at Hotel 'I' in Zagreb, and the Regional Control Centre was in Brdo near Kranj. Aircraft, necessary for their tasks in the geographically complex terrain and for quick transportation, were provided by the Netherlands as its participation in the EC mission.

On 15 July, the first part of the staff arrived at Pleso airport, and on 18 July, three SA.316B Alouette III helicopters (numbers A 301, A 343, and A 451) from the 298th Squadron of the Royal Netherlands Air Force (*Koninklijke Luchtmacht*) landed. Four experienced pilots, four technicians, and one logistics officer were selected for the Balkan mission. The detachment's base was on the civilian side of Pleso, temporarily moved to Brnik in Slovenia for security reasons. Pilots carried out high-risk observation tasks above the battlefield, and liaison duties.

Due to the nature of their mission, Alouette III helicopters were painted white with large text 'EC Monitoring Mission' for immediate identification from the ground. Visibility did not guarantee safety, and there were several incidents where Alouette III helicopters were targeted. On 16 August, A 343 was hit with five rounds, one piercing the main rotor blade. Later, Dutch pilots noticed that they were under anti-aircraft (AA) gun fire on a number of occasions. On an assignment on 9 October, it was observed that shots were fired at an Alouette III and the next day a technician found a hole from a 7.62mm round in the engine cover.

The ECMM support tasks mainly involved observation and transportation, including flights for VIPs coming for negotiations with the warring parties.

The Alouette III's crew consisted of one pilot and one technician, who also served as a navigator. Before the detachment's departure to the Balkans, three Navstar GPS 100 Global Positioning Systems were procured and provisionally attached to the instrument panel. Navigation was challenging in 1991, as GPS was far from perfect, especially in mountainous terrain and complex meteorological conditions.

From 1 October, the ECMM air fleet was reinforced with the arrival of the Italian *Aviazione leggera dell'Esercito* detachment, consisting of one AB.205 and two AB.206B Jet Ranger III helicopters, along with 21 staff members. The Italians had their first engagement on 3 October when their AB.205B on a flight from Zagreb to Rijeka was hit by two 7.62mm rounds.

Three months after the Brioni Declaration, on 7 October, Slovenia formally severed ties with the SFRJ. One consequence was the introduction of a requirement to announce flights by the ECMM 48 hours before execution. The mission's jurisdiction in Slovenia was suspended on 13 October, and flights continued over Croatia.

The first rotation for the Dutch staff ended on 9 October, and the second group took over the task without a change in equipment. For security reasons, the Dutch government decided on 22 October to withdraw all personnel and Alouette III helicopters from the field, and they flew back home the next day.

Dutch Alouette III in flight over Zagreb on a liaison mission for the ECMM (NIMH)

During the initial battles, there was no effective Combat Search and Rescue (C-SAR). Based on experience from a series of shootdowns, it was suggested to organise C-SAR with Mi-8s and combat teams from the 63rd Parachute Brigade, and for these to be on standby near the area of the action. These were ordered to closely monitor friendly radio communications because it was an effective way to immediately inform C-SAR about incidents and to go to their Mi-8s.

Air Force Planning

As much as the JNA was always considered a pillar of the existence, sovereignty, and territorial integrity of the SFRJ, the separation of Slovenia and Croatia caught it, literally, unprepared. The only concrete war plan that the JNA had for the kind of scenario that developed in Croatia during the second half of 1991, was a cobbled together idea about lifting the blockade of certain units and institutions.[4]

Eventually, the ŠVK ordered the launch of an offensive against the cities where the barracks and warehouses were surrounded, but which were mostly outside the populated areas. In these battles, the RV i PVO was engaged according to Plan Krilo (Wing), most often at the call of the land forces for operations against selected targets that threatened the blockaded units or were in the way of the forces sent to lift the blockades. Planned actions were mainly battlefield air interdiction against concentrations of forces in the enemy rear, or movements towards the line of separation, and also against bridges and TV and radio transmitters.

For the offensives, Kadijević's original plan to cut Croatia into several parts was drastically modified: indeed, reduced to breakthroughs to major JNA units blockaded by the opposition.[5] According to his subsequent interpretation in his memoirs after the war, the main reason for the change of plans was the poorly implemented mobilisation and the desertion of some of the reservists. At the time, when active combat operations began, the mobilisation recalled around 105,000 reservists: however, some 15,000 defected soon after and only around 90,000 were left.

Arguably, the JNA and RV i PVO already had around 136,000 officers and other ranks under arms. However, when units deployed in other parts of the SFRJ, various institutions, and the units responsible for protection of borders were excluded – only some 30,000 troops ready for action remained. However, Kadijević's plan required the deployment of about 250,000 troops. Therefore, the JNA and the RV i PVO found themselves 130,000 troops short of what was considered necessary to fulfil the plan. Unsurprisingly, many of the mobilised units sent to Croatia quickly became demoralised because they found themselves understaffed and confused.[6] By comparison, Croatia mobilised its full defence effectives and was never short of troops.

Organisation of the RV i PVO as of September 1991

As of September 1991, the Command and Control of the RV i PVO was divided between I Corps RV i PVO, to which the majority of aviation units were directly subordinated, and the 1st Military District (MD), which was responsible for operations in East Slavonija, Dalmatija (Dalmatia), and southern Croatia. Combat units subordinated to these two commands were based at Batajnica (outside Beograd), Ortiješ and Golubovci (all three in Serbia), and in Tuzla (northern Bosnia). However, the western part of the battlefield was under the control of the 5th MD, which had its own, directly subordinated, flying units, all assigned to V Corps RV i PVO. These were the 117th Aviation Brigade (distributed at air bases in Bihać and Banja Luka), the 105th Fighter-Bomber Aviation Regiment (based at Udbina and tasked with operations in Dalmatia), and the 111th Aviation Brigade (reformed into a regiment effective from 6 October 1991). All units received reinforcements from III Corps RV i PVO: for example, a squadron each was sent to Pula and Tuzla Air Bases (ABs), while units not engaged in combat operations continued their routine training.

The fighting in Croatia culminated in October, by when the RV i PVO was carrying out 50–60 combat missions every day. Due to the shape of Croatia, which is elongated in the form of a croissant, parts of the battlefield were relatively clearly demarcated. The battles were fought in the geographical war zones of Eastern Slavonia, Western Slavonia, Kordun and Banija, Lika, northern Dalmatia and southern Dalmatia.

On the other hand, the JNA's intact and operational formations were gravitating around the parts of Croatia closest to Serbia – Eastern Slavonia – where they fought under the command of the 1st MD. V Corps had the leading role in Western Slavonia, in Kordun and Banija, while X Corps was responsible for Dalmatia, and IX

A Jastreb from 252nd Squadron taking off on a combat mission from Batajnica in summer 1991 armed with a typical combat load for CAS missions of two 57mm rocket pods and four 5-inch HVAR rockets. (Dragan Veličković)

Corps for Lika (unlike Croatian forces which were organised on a natural geographical basis).[7]

The involvement of the RV i PVO is presented in this book in the same geographic order, region by region: which was also constrained by the limited tactical radius of the aircraft they were operating, its units focussed on tasks in areas in proximity to their bases.

Croatian Air Defences

At the beginning of the war, in the summer of 1991, the Croatian defences used a small number of AA guns, predominantly of 20mm calibre (the smallest calibre still classified as a 'gun'). On paper, but not in reality, every brigade of the Croat National Guard (*Zbor narodne garde*, ZNG) was to have an air defence company with two single-barrel PAT 20mm AA guns, and 30 launchers for Soviet-made Strela-2M MANPADS (ASCC/NATO-reporting name 'SA-7 Grail'). Additionally, each of the same brigade's infantry battalions was supposed to have six Strela-2Ms. Actually, the composition of individual brigades and their battalions varied greatly and usually depended on what kind of weapons they were able to capture from the JNA or the stocks of the Territorial Defence (*Territorijalna obrana*, TO). However, as described in Volume 1, following an order from Beograd in 1990, all equipment of the TO was collected and stored under the control of the JNA. Thus, it was rather a matter of luck for a few units to receive some support from private persons that managed to smuggle in a variety of other weapons from abroad. That said, in general it can be said that most of the Croat brigades did not even have symbolic air defences. For example, the 'best' outfitted Croat unit early during the war – the Tuškanac-based 1st Guard Brigade – had only two 20/3 M55 three-barrel, and two 20/1 M55J single-barrel 20mm guns, and a few Strela-2Ms on hand. These weapons were also all the Croats could use to protect such vital installations in Zagreb as the buildings housing its government, the Parliament, the buildings of the Croatian national TV stations, several large industrial zones around Zagreb, and the TV repeater at Mount Sljeme, a mountain towering above the country's capital.[8]

That said, the Croats had lots of troops with extensive military service in the JNA, and in some cases had captured equipment forgotten in long-abandoned warehouses. This, for example, was the case with several German-made 20mm Flak 38s left over from the Second World War and which were available both in the single- and twin-barrelled versions. Of similar quality were about 40 Bofors L/60 40mm guns found in warehouses in various ports on the Adriatic Sea. On the other hand, the number of Yugoslav-made 20mm guns was minimal. For example, on 20 July 1991, the 108th TO Brigade in Slavonski Brod acquired six M55 guns from the Đuro Đaković factory, where also the principal Yugoslav main battle tanks – M-84s (a licenced version of the Soviet-designed T-72M) – were manufactured. Around the same time, two batteries equipped with M55Js came into being at the compound of the Sisak Ironworks. Unsurprisingly, the discovery of about 80 Browning M2 12.7mm/0.50-cal heavy machine guns at the Technical Works in Bregana was a major gem, because these powerful weapons with their high rate of fire were almost as effective as M55s.

According to Tus, the spoils of the 'Blockade of the Barracks' – of blockades and assaults on JNA bases in Croatia between September and November 1991 – were immense. The Croats obtained over 200,000 infantry weapons and over 500,000 tons of various ammunition, 250 tanks, 320 armoured fighting vehicles, 630 artillery systems, 780 anti-tank systems, and – amongst others – over 500 AA guns and MANPADs. In Đakovo, for example, the Croatians captured 18 BOV-3 20/3 self-propelled AA guns (with triple 20mm AA guns), one self-propelled M-53/59 (Czechoslovak-manufactured twin 30mm AA guns), 12 towed 20mm M-55 20/3 AA guns, and 104 Strela-2M MANPADs. In Varaždin barracks, Croatian forces captured four Strela-1M self-propelled surface-to-air missile (SAM) launchers (ASCC/NATO-reporting name 'SA-9 Gaskin') with 94 missiles, 33 grips for Strela-2M MANPADS and 186 missiles, 11 BOV-3s, and eight 20mm M75 AA guns. Finally, the Croats assumed control over the Rade Končar Works in Zagreb, which were working on launching production of the Strela-10M under licence from the USSR. There, they found three self-propelled launchers for these, including one each of the 9A34M and 9A35M, and a Yugoslav version of the system, mounted on the chassis of the M-80A infantry fighting vehicle (IFV). Therefore, in a matter of just a few days in September 1991, the Croats obtained 380 MANPADs and short-range air defence systems (SHORADs), and 130 AA guns of various calibres.

That said, the Croat operations were largely conducted without effective overall control. According to Zvonimir Ambrinac, an air defence officer that left the JNA and – from mid-May 1991 onwards – served as one of the organisers of the artillery and air defence of the ZNG:

> ...resulting in the disorganised seizure of weapons and equipment. It happened that a cannon was taken from its own warehouse, and it was not known who took it nor where. Citizens carried Strela-2M missile launchers without even knowing what they were. Many launchers were discarded when those who took them out of storage realised that they could not use them.[9]

Nevertheless, through September 1991, the ZNG did manage to build-up a robust short-range air defence system. This called upon a well-organised network for reporting aircraft movements. The point was that the majority of RV i PVO air bases – like those in Udbina, Zemunik, Bihać, Mahovljani, Mostar and Tuzla – were in the proximity of areas with Croat populations. People from the areas in question organised a network of collaborators that closely tracked all activities of the air force, and forwarded relevant reports to the crisis HQs at municipal levels, responsible for organising observation and reconnaissance. Additionally, the ZNG established its own network of observation posts.

Intelligence gathering for the RV i PVO, on the other hand, became a major issue. Whether due to the mass exodus of personnel, its exposure to various forms of outside influence, or because the personnel were locked within its bases, busy maintaining a high rate of combat readiness, or taking care of their families and those of other military professionals, the air force proved unable to collect intelligence on its own. Indeed, its personnel experienced very intense psychological and propagandist pressure, and the fear for naked survival significantly eroded its morale. Croatian intelligence not only gained access to personal data about officers and other ranks but also accessed confidential documentation about the relocation of units, and any changes in the staff of all the units. It further leveraged this through various forms of clandestine activities, including offers of high salaries for commanders ready to defect, soft offers for ensuring protection, and also open threats and intimidation of family members. Unsurprisingly, an analysis of the RV i PVO in combat of 1991 openly concluded that the circumstances were such that the service learned about the Croatian force primarily through open-source intelligence (OSINT) – such as reporting in the media

– while 'they knew everything about us, even what we did not know ourselves'.[10]

Finally, the RV i PVO initially applied entirely wrong tactics: essentially the same as in training during peacetime. Pilots tended to enter the combat zone at much too high an altitude and, after making their strafing or bombing runs, would pull up to high altitude – although still within the envelope of enemy weapons. They also tended to make multiple attack runs. Unsurprisingly, one of the first related analyses by the RV i PVO concluded that pilots had to learn to make only one attack run and then exit the combat zone as soon as possible in order to avoid the effects of enemy air defences. This was actually something the doctrine of the air force had been teaching since the Arab-Israeli War of June 1967 but had meanwhile been completely forgotten.

The most effective means of Croatian air defence against Yugoslav aircraft were Strela-2M MANPADS, which were mostly spoils of war from the stockpiles of the JNA. The destruction zone with that system was 2,800m in distance and up to 2,300m in altitude. (Boris Gregurić)

An 9M35M launch vehicle for the Strela-10M deployed for action in the city centre of Zagreb in September 1991. (Boris Gregurić)

2
QUICK COLLAPSE IN THE NORTH

On the maps, Croatia resembles a crescent-shaped pastry. As of 1991–1992, and clockwise, its geographic regions were known as Medjimurje and Zagorje (in the north), Turopolje, Banija and Kordun (centre); Podravina, Bilogora, Moslavina, and Posavina (also 'Western Slavonia'), Slavonija and Baranja with Srijem/Srem (east); mountainous Gorski Kotar and Lika; the Istra (or Istrian) Peninsula, and Dalmacija (much of the Adriatic coast and its hinterland). While geographically close to each other, many of these areas were separated by the local terrain and an underdeveloped road network. For example: in the north, the Drava River separated the Medjimurje region from the Varaždin area and the Zagorje region, which in turn was separated from the Zagreb area by Mount Sljeme. Podravina – the area along the Drava River that also marked the border between Yugoslavia and Hungary – was separated from the area further south by the Bilogora hills, while another chain of hills separated the latter from the Moslavina Region. Posavina was the area along the Sava River, which – just like the Drava River in the north – is a tributary to the Danube: the latter marked the eastern border of Croatia, and its easternmost region: Slavonija. Central Croatia included the regions of Turopolje, Banija, and Kordun (the latter two had predominantly Serbian population) – three regions with gradually elevating high plateaus – bordered by the mountains of the Gorski Kotar in the west, and the Dinara Alps in the east. Istra, the peninsula in the west, was thus geographically separated from the rest of the country. The same was true for the regions of Lika (another area predominantly populated by Serbs), and the coastal region of Dalmacija.

This geography also dictated the Federal ground operations of the second half of 1991, and is how the story of RV i PVO operations will be reconstructed as well.

Drama in Bjelovar

One unit of RV i PVO located in the town of Bjelovar, in the Bilogora region, was doomed right from the start of the Croatian blockade of the Federal bases: the 1st Air Surveillance Company was home-based in the northern part of the town, in the settlement known as Zvijerci. Equipped with the old, British-made Marconi S-600 radar, this unit was directly subordinated to the 5th Air Surveillance Regiment. The survival of this small unit in an extremely aggressive environment was unsustainable, and thus during the armed conflict in Slovenia, on 29 June 1991 the regiment's command requested relocation from the Command of the V Corps RV i PVO to one of the reserve radar sites. No approval was granted and during the battles for the military bases in Bjelovar, the 1st Company became an easy target. Its commander was ordered that in the event of an open attack, he should destroy vital parts of the radar system and break out from his isolated base to the huge Božidar Adžija barracks, closer to the town, which housed the entire 265th Mechanised Brigade.

However, on 29 September 1991, Croatian forces relatively quickly seized the main base, capturing nearly all of the heavy equipment of the 265th Brigade, including dozens of T-55 main battle tanks (MBTs), old M36 General Jackson self-propelled anti-tank guns, and ZSU-57-2 self-propelled AA guns. The commander of the garrison requested air strikes, but nothing happened. This left the radar operators without hope. They surrendered on the condition that they would all be allowed to go home. Together with the remaining prisoners of war they were transferred to the barracks and lined up to witness the execution of the commander of the 265th Brigade and two other officers. The reason the Croats were so vengeful was that during their attack on the *Barutana* – a large ammunition depot in the forest of Bedenik, one kilometre west of Bjelovar, and surrounded by the village of Hrgovljani – a Serb officer detonated an explosive charge to prevent the capture of 1,700 tons of ammunition.

A map of the traditional geographic regions of Croatia as of 1991. (Map by Tom Cooper)

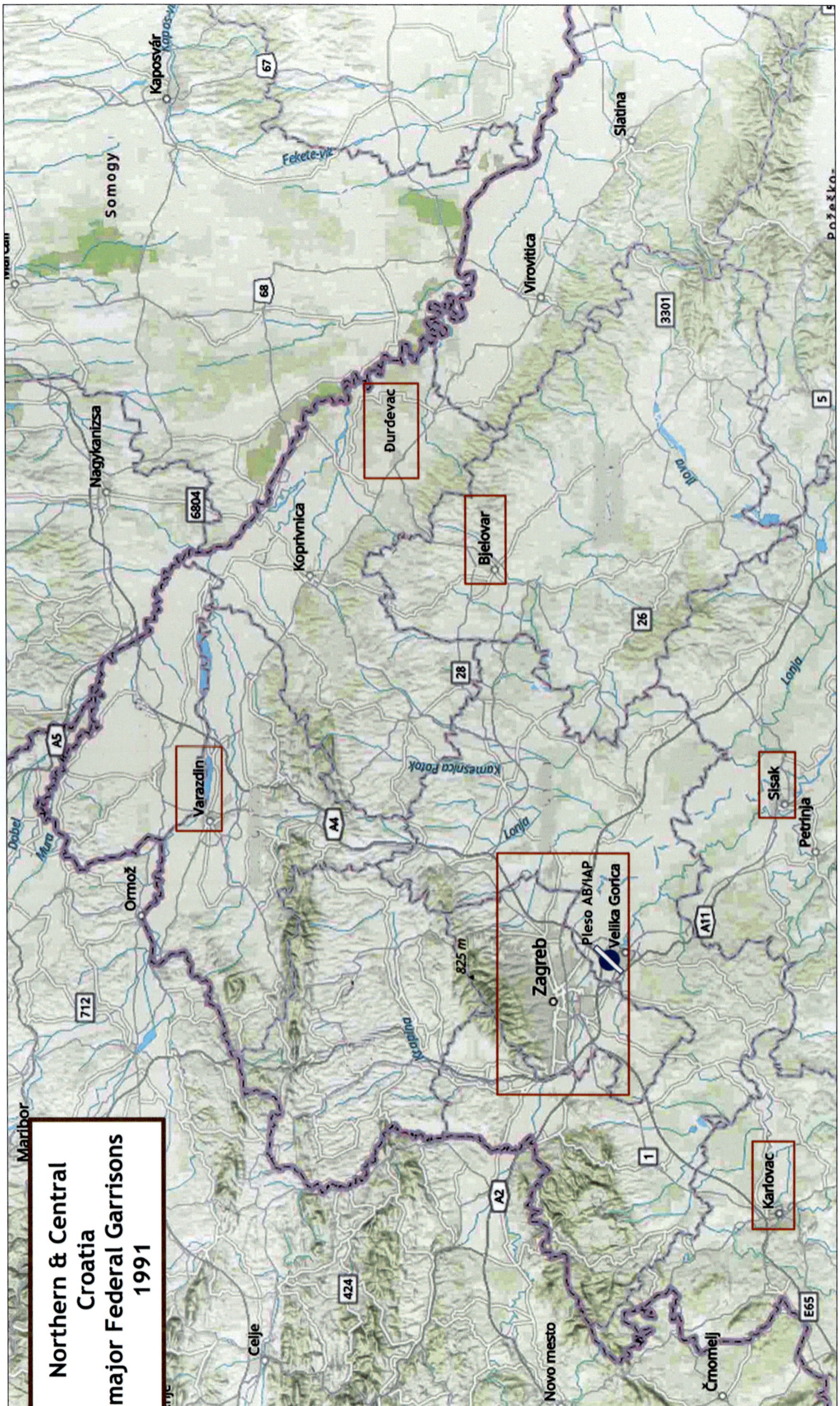

(Map by Tom Cooper)

The result was a detonation comparable to that of a small nuclear bomb, killing not only 11 Croat troops, but also destroying or badly damaging nearly all the houses in Hrgovljani, and wounding dozens. Eventually, members of the local crisis staff allowed the release of the radar operators. The rest of the Croatian war spoils in the base of the 1st Company included the control cabin of the S-605C, four 20/3 AA guns, and two towed quad 12.7mm machine guns. [1]

The Federal Garrison of Zagreb

During the summer of 1991, due to the growing tensions the main command of the 5th MD, one of the three strategic groupings of the JNA, was transferred from the centre of Zagreb to the Slunj range, more than 80km to the south. Generals and high-ranking officers were in secure locations, but in the narrower core of the city of Zagreb and its broader surroundings, a significant number of institutions and units of the JNA remained surrounded. This included the Command of the JNA's X Corps and units that relied on the 140th Mechanised Brigade of X Corps, located in the Maršal Tito barracks. Parts of the brigade and its headquarters were in the village of Dugo, east of Zagreb. The main part of the 4th Armoured Brigade of X Corps was located in Jastrebarsko, a town southwest of Zagreb.

From the point of view of the RV i PVO, the most important element deployed in Croatia was the AS-84. Developed within the framework of Project Bacchus by Marconi of Great Britain to Yugoslav requirements, this computer-supported automated tactical management system (ATMS) was introduced to service in 1988–1989 and operated by the 5th Regiment RV i PVO headquartered at Pleso AB. The AS-84 was capable of simultaneously tracking up to 400 different aircraft and helicopters, coordinating the work of dozens of radar stations, selecting targets, and controlling the work of airborne- and ground-based air defences with maximum efficiency. On 10 July 1991, the RV i PVO managed to evacuate its elements from Pleso AB to Bihać AB. Its renewed installation and establishment of solid lines of communications to all the subordinated elements took time, and the AS-84 was declared operational again only on 15 September 1991. From that point onwards, it played a crucial role in the command and control of V Corps of the RV i PVO, enabling its headquarters to exercise effective control of the battle from its new command post in Klek, near Bihać AB.[2]

That said, the headquarters of V Corps, the command and some elements of the 5th Air Surveillance Regiment, ground crews of the 111th Aviation Brigade, and the 149th Medium Self-Propelled Air Defence Missile Regiment – equipped with Kub-M (ASCC/NATO-reporting name 'SA-6 Gainful') surface-to-air missiles (SAMs) – remained at Pleso AB (officially designated the 151st Air Base by the RV i PVO).[3] This crucial facility was defended by the 151st Light Air Defence Artillery and Missile Battalion (including Bofors 40mm L/70 AA guns and 20mm M55A4B1 AA guns), several smaller units of the JNA, the Sabotage Detachment of the 65th Motorised Regiment, three T-55A MBTs and seven M-80 IFVs from the 140th Mechanised Brigade, and a task force from the 63rd Parachute Brigade. During the blockade of Pleso AB, lacking any kind of aerial threats, the majority of the officers and other ranks of the RV i PVO garrisoned there had to serve as infantry: each unit was assigned a different sector of the defence perimeter. Paratroopers served as a rapid reaction force. In addition to the air base, they also had to protect the Zmaj Works, at Nova Gorica: one of three major overhaul facilities of the air force.

The plan of the 5th MD was for the units in the city and surrounding areas to defend and prepare for an organised breakout to meet units coming from the south-east. On 19 September 1991, at 0500hrs, Task Force-1 (*Operativna grupa*, OG-1) was ordered to engage. This force included the 622nd Motorised Brigade (XIII Corps) and reinforcements from central Serbia – specifically the 544th Motorised Brigade from the Šabac garrison and the 169th Motorised Brigade from the Loznica garrison, along with a tank battalion from the 51st Mechanised Brigade – one tank company from the 329th Armoured Brigade, and the TO units of Kordun and Banija. Their task was to break the Croatian armed forces in battles along the main axis of Bečuga–Petrinja–Lekenik, with additional support along the secondary axis of Vojnić–Karlovac. In the initial phase, the JNA aimed to reach the Kupa River on the Petrinja–Karlovac line, then extend offensives along the Petrinja–Lekenik–Velika Gorica (Pleso AB) axis to lift the blockade of the Karlovac garrison and facilitate the withdrawal of forces from Zagreb. A task force with artillery and multiple rocket launchers (MRLs) – Military Artillery Group-5 (*Vojišna artiljerijska grupa*, VAG-5) – was formed. For actions in depth up to 68km, Military Rocket Group-5 (*Vojišna raketna grupa*, VRG-5) was established, consisting of the 389th Rocket Brigade from Banja Luka equipped with the 9K52 Luna-M system (ASCC/NATO codename 'Frog-7').

As OG-1 approached Zagreb according to the plan of the 5th MD, it was expected that the 140th Mechanised Brigade would leave the city and breakout to the suburb of Velika Gorica, pulling members of all other units and institutions with them. Subsequently, all these forces were to withdraw from the endangered area along the Petrinja–Dvor–Bosanski Novi (now Novi Grad) axis.

For the parts of the 4th Armoured Brigade that were under blockade, the 5th MD ordered them to breakout along the Jastrebarsko–Donja Zdenčina axis, join up with the 367th Signal Regiment there (which was supposed to exit the barracks in Samobor, west of Zagreb, under combat conditions), and then both units, with the support of aviation and artillery, were to exit the combat zone along the Donja Zdenčina–Lasinja–Vrginmost axis.

The plan for the aviation was to carry out 'strong air attacks on the cities of Zagreb, Karlovac, Jastrebarsko and Samobor and to participate in the fire support of break through efforts'; to support the main forces of OG-1 (along the Petrinja–Velika Gorica axis) and the breakout and withdrawal of forces from the garrisons of Zagreb and Samobor in the direction of Zagreb–Velika Gorica–Petrinja and the villages of Samobor and Zdenčina of Lasinje–Vrginmost; with part of the force to support the withdrawal of forces from the Bjelovar area in the direction of Bjelovar–Daruvar.[4] In accordance with the development of the situation, to support the breakthrough and extraction of forces of XIV Corps from Slovenia in the direction of Ljubljana–Novo Mesto–Karlovac.[5]

From the Croatian perspective, there was a perceived high risk of an airborne assault by the JNA on Pleso airport and the connection of those forces with Maršal Tito barracks. In such case, the massive volumes of equipment stored at the later base, for the lack of personnel, would be put to use by the Serbs. An additional concern was the fact that the front line on the Kupa River was only about 20km from Pleso: obviously, the JNA had the potential to cross the river and close a 'ring of fire around Zagreb' in the event of a breakthrough towards Jastrebarsko and Dugo Selo. Vedriš, the chief of the city's crisis HQ, also feared a breakthrough along the Karlovac–Jastrebarsko–Pleso axis into the centre of Croatia and an advance into the heart of Zagreb. That is why various obstacles were set up around the barracks and city roads, including tanks with diesel, gas, and petrol. The goal was to thwart any attempt at a breakthrough.

Meanwhile, a cat-and-mouse game was being played. The defenders of the city put the JNA barracks under massive pressure, while President Tuđman was easing tensions through negotiations with military leaders, Belgrade, and the international community. Vedriš recalled: 'When Tuđman ordered us to ease up, we would obey, but for three, four days, the barracks would once again be left without electricity and water'.[6]

Assigned to support Pleso and other barracks were aviation units under the control of V Corps of the RV i PVO, including the 117th Aviation Brigade from Bihać and the 105th Fighter-Bomber Aviation Regiment from the base at Udbina.

First Air Defences of the Croatian Capital

On the first day of the complete blockade of the JNA bases in the Zagreb area, on 13 September 1991, at around 1945hrs, two MiG-21bis aircraft took-off from the Quick Reaction Alert (QRA) in Bihać, forcing a Croatian Airlines MD-82 to land at Pleso. Two weeks prior to this incident, a shipment of assault rifles was found on a Boeing 707, which was forced to land at Pleso (see Volume 1 for details). The RV i PVO considered this not to be an isolated incident and anticipated additional shipments. Passenger planes were consequently grounded and forced to the military part of the airport. After a thorough search, they were allowed to continue their flights.

According to Croatian data, the first registered case of overflight of the city occurred on 15 September when a flight of two MiG-21bis aircraft triggered an air raid alert. Actually, the aircraft were conducting a show of force. The next day, the aircraft attacked the 169-metre Sljeme TV tower, which stands on top of Mount Medvednica, north of Zagreb. From low altitude, they fired six unguided rockets, hitting the area with the generator, causing a fire in the TV tower building, which was extinguished.

During the night from 15 to 16 September, commander of the V Corps of the RV i PVO, Bajić, ordered the relocation of his command from Pleso to Bihać:

> I ordered the engagement of eight Mi-8 helicopters from my 111th Aviation Brigade, and reliable and expert crews were selected. The night was dark with no moonlight. Flights began half an hour after midnight with a half-hour interval between take-offs. Pilots did not turn on lights and flew on different courses and altitudes to confuse the Croatian armed forces. This continued up to the Kupa River, which at that time separated our and their forces. Around 160 people were transferred during the night, and I was in the second-to-last group.

Due to the importance of the capital city, Croatian forces made efforts to organise air defences in multiple layers around the city perimeter. Initially, the core of these forces consisted of a few remaining AA guns from the TO that had evaded JNA control during the collection of weapons in May 1990. In the Elka factory, which produced electronics and cables, a 40mm M1 Bofors AA gun and approximately 20 cases of ammunition were found. It was retrieved from the factory on 28 August and transported to a suburban settlement, where a unit was formed and filled with volunteers from the Dubrava District, later known as the Armed Detachment of the National Protection.[7]

The potential for air defence sharply increased after the fall of the Duboki Jarak warehouse, located in the easternmost quarter of Zagreb, where a large quantity of weapons belonging to the TO unit of the city of Zagreb was stored. At dawn of 14 September, Croat forces blockaded the warehouse with anti-tank obstacles set up on the roads and intersections. They opened fire on the JNA guard, equivalent to a platoon, which returned fire. Every half hour, the warehouse crew was called upon by loudspeaker to 'surrender the weapons, which belong to the Croatian people. After three and a half days, the warehouse crew reached an agreement to surrender the warehouse on the condition that they could safely transfer with their personal weapons to the main Zagreb Maršal Tito barracks, which was a strong JNA 'fortress'.[8]

The Command of V Corps of the RV i PVO ordered the 229th Squadron of the 185th Regiment (Pula AB) to attack the facility with eight Galeb-4 aircraft, each armed with four L-128-04MD M74 Munja unguided rockets, in addition to their GSh-23 gun pods. However, the regiment's commander, Lieutenant Colonel Marijan Vratović, explained:

> I consciously did not want the pilots to carry out the task, even though I had all the data on the positions of the warehouses that I was supposed to target. I ordered the pilots to search for a warehouse along the route from Dugo Selo to Vrbovec [in the wrong direction; author's note]. As they did not find the specified warehouses, they returned without completing the mission.[9]

In Duboki Jarak, Croats acquired around 13,000 assault rifles, approximately 100 guns and mortars, around 80 cross-country vehicles, and air defence ordnance. The resulting air defence unit received 12 Strela-2M gripstocks with 22 missiles, one 20mm AA gun, and 12.7mm/.50-cal Browning M2HB machine gun, along with significant quantities of 40mm and 20mm ammunition. The atmosphere at that time was reflected in the rapid exchange of equipment too: the city headquarters provided the Dubrava battery with a three-barrel AA gun in exchange for its single-barrel weapon, while half the Strela-2Ms were handed over to other units. The battery was then redeployed to three positions in the eastern parts of Zagreb: two Strela-2M teams at St Barbara, two Strela-2M teams atop the tallest buildings in the city, and the rest in Pionirski Grad, to provide air defences for the base of III Battalion, 1st Guards Brigade of the ZNG. Additional support came in the form of a SNAR-10 artillery radar (ASCC/NATO-reporting name 'Big Fred'): this was actually of minimal use but great symbolic importance.[10]

CAPTURED Mi-8

On 22 September 1991, a Mi-8 serial number 12271, from the 780th Squadron, took-off from Bihać AB with the task of evacuating wounded from Pleso AB. Flying at a very low altitude, the crew of three managed to reach the village of Brest – outside Mala Gorica – when it encountered troops of the IV Battalion, 1st Guards Brigade of the ZNG. Warned by the sound of the approaching helicopter, at around 14.45hrs, the Croats quickly set up an ambush and opened fire as the helicopter was passing just 30 metres above them.[11]

Due to multiple hits, the crew of the Mi-8 was forced to make an emergency landing in an area under the control of Croatian forces. One pilot was slightly injured, while the second pilot and technician escaped without injuries. All three crew members became prisoners of war and were later exchanged, while the Mi-8 became the property of the Croatian armed forces.

Upon receiving the news that a Mi-8 had made an emergency landing near Petrinja, Vladimir Bagarić, a pilot from the 780th Squadron who had deserted in June 1991, went to the scene. At the time, he was responsible for monitoring the radio communications of the JNA:

> We found the Mi-8 in a cornfield, riddled with small arms fire, with a hundred holes, pierced fuel tanks leaking, but no vital part was damaged. By the time we arrived, locals had taken off some parts, including the battery, so we couldn't turn on the avionics and see what was functioning. At the same time, our guys at Pleso airport, held by the JNA, managed to steal two generators with which we were able to start the engines.

Following emergency repairs, a Croat crew of two pilots and one technician evacuated the helicopter to Lučko, flying by night and with all lights turned off. The Mi-8 crew was running low on fuel and could not wait, so before landing they turned on the signal lights: when those on the ground recognised them, the airfield was well-illuminated, and the helicopter landed safely. The future Croatian Air Force thus received its first operational Mi-8.[12]

Crisis on the Ground

That said, the main events of the following drama took place on the ground and were primarily related to the blockade of several bases. In just the city centre, the Croatian forces blockaded no fewer than 30 different military facilities: the majority of smaller barracks with minimal occupants surrendered rather quickly. From the infrastructure of the RV i PVO, this included the Command of V Corps (with around 55 officers and other ranks), and the 298th Signal Battalion (based at the small airfield of Lučko in the suburbs of Zagreb), where eight officers, 12 NCOs, and 87 soldiers surrendered on 16 September. Only four managed to escape across the field to the base of the 155th Regiment in Kerestinec. The Croatian spoils included four AA guns, around 350 assault rifles, and assorted grenades, ammunition, and vehicles.[13]

Closer to the city, Kurilovec radar station, of the combined civilian-military District Air Traffic Control, was guarded by 17 soldiers from the 5th Regiment. On 16 September, it was approached by several Croats, but the commander refused to surrender although civilians working at the station all fled. The next day, 1st Sergeant Slobodan Dostanić attempted to drive to Pleso AB, to pick up food, but was apprehended. After being released on demand of the 5th Regiment, he disappeared. Down to Sergeant 1st Class Ivan Dobranski, the small garrison remained isolated, sometimes exposed to fire: its members searched their warehouse and found a sack each of flour and old beans. This was enough to feed them for a few days longer. The Croats thus resorted to emotional pressure and on 20 September approached the main gate accompanied by Dobranski's wife: she was allowed to walk in and spent the night inside the compound, refusing to leave unless he did. Left with little choice, Dobranski surrendered around 1300hrs of the following day. Now only the young Sergeant Đorđe Radvanski remained, who had just arrived from school. The guard was divided on whether to fight or surrender. Radvanski retained command and strengthened his authority. On 22 September, he received support from aviation in an attack at 1455hrs. The Croatian unit conducting the blockade of the radar post was hit by two jets of the RV i PVO: one of their unguided 57mm rockets hit their position, killing one Croatian soldier and injuring another, and setting fire to a hangar and several cars nearby. Immediately after, a ceasefire was agreed, and the garrison was permitted to leave, accompanied by two guard dogs and escorted by the police to Pleso AB, where they arrived around 1900hrs. Before leaving, they sabotaged the radar, two 20/3 AA guns, and two Browning machine guns.[14]

The situation was much better at Pleso AB, which was regularly resupplied by Mi-8s of the 780th Squadron, operating from Bihać AB: even as of early October 1991, the Croats in the Zagreb area had troops but next to no weapons, and even less ammunition. Certainly enough, they were continuously establishing ever more units, but these lacked equipment. For example, the pretentiously named 50th Air Defence Regiment, responsible for air defence of southern Zagreb from 3 October 1991, had only one AA gun per battalion. The unsurprising result was the decision to seize some of the bases. First, the Croats focussed on those in the Samobor area, where the 367th Signal Regiment of the JNA was guarding the equipment of no fewer than five TO brigades. The attack on this base was launched in the late afternoon of 6 October 1991. Facing stiff resistance, the attack went on into the night: around midnight, the Strela-1M team deployed at Nedeljski Breg was informed about an incoming air strike and advised to quickly redeploy. Shortly after, its former position was targeted with the use of flare bombs. The Croats fired back but without success.

Eventually, the 367th Signal Regiment – which had meanwhile lost one soldier killed – surrendered to the Croatian police early the next morning. By then, two out of four large hangars storing arms and ammunition had been completely destroyed, thus denying the Croats about 8,000 out of about 16,000 firearms and a number of AA guns.

The defence positions of the base at Pleso were in some places near the first houses. Most participants in those events remember the pressure they felt due to the fact that they were involved in the civil war and were fighting against people who were their fellow citizens in Zagreb. Signs indicating that the area was mined were placed on the fences. (Aleksandar Radić collection)

Antonov An-26 aircraft flew between Pleso, which was surrounded, and Batajnica, but only after the ceasefire from mid-November 1991. (Vilijam Horvat)

One of the notable officers in the defence of the base at Pleso was Lieutenant Veljko Kajtazi (on the right), who served in the Air Technical Service. He is a characteristic example of personal fate in the division of the SFRJ; a Roma from Kosovo who initially served as an NCO and later completed the academy to become an officer. He left the JNA in 1992 and became a civilian in Croatia, where he was a teacher in electrical engineering at a school. Since 2011, he has been a member of the parliament as a representative of one of the 12 national minorities. (Vilijam Horvat)

A MiG-23ML with Iraqi markings remained stranded while on overhaul at the Zmaj plant, an extension of Pleso AB. The test pilot for MiGs, Major Omer Avdaković, remembers his favourite MiG-23ML, number 23269, which was the leading aircraft of the 10 received for overhaul from Iraq in 1989. Avdaković wanted to retrieve his aircraft and explored possibilities for a sudden take-off from a taxiway instead of a runway. He quickly drove along the taxiways by car to check the length and conditions in the vicinity. He estimated that a taxiway of 650 metres would be sufficient to get airborne and initiate the climb. For such a flight, he relied on the noise of the tank engines to mask the start of the aircraft engine. The challenge was the positions of the Croatian air defences that he had to fly over immediately after take-off. The order to take-off was not given until an agreement on the peaceful relocation of the plant was reached in December 1991. In the meantime, days passed with constant exposure to the blockade of the base and occasional small arms fire from Croatian forces. (Milorad Ristić)

A MiG-21bis from Bihać going on a mission armed, as was usual in the autumn of 1991, with only two pods for 57mm unguided rockets. (Milorad Ristić)

ATTACK WITH A MAVERICK MISSILE

The radio and TV repeater tower on Mount Sljeme was considered a valuable target, and thus the RV i PVO decided to knock it out using precious US-made AGM-65B Maverick electro-optically guided air-to-surface missiles, only modest quantities of which were available. Indeed, out of some 212 acquired in 1983, only some 207 were in storage, and merely a handful of J-22 Orao fighter-bombers were equipped with the installations necessary for their deployment. 238th Squadron – the unit nominally responsible for the Zagreb area – had none, and thus, it received two J-22s – serial numbers 25172 and 25173 (both equipped with afterburners) – from the 241st Squadron in Banja Luka.

On 4 October, the two jets took-off from the base and approached Zagreb at an altitude of 5,000 metres. The leader flew serial number 25172: after failing to acquire the target on his first two passes, he managed to obtain a lock-on during the third and fired a single AGM-65B. The pull-up from the dive began at an altitude of 2,500 metres and speed of 630km/h, with afterburners engaged. While pulling a hard, 4g turn towards the sun and climbing to around 2,800 metres, the pilot felt an impact at the rear of the jet. The right engine immediately failed, but, using the left one, he managed to climb to an altitude of 4,000 metres and then return to Banja Luka, without major difficulties except for severe vibrations. After manually lowering the landing gear, he landed safely. The post-flight inspection revealed that the Orao had been hit by a Strela-2M, which wrecked the turbine components and the combustion chamber of the right engine, damaged the right horizontal stabiliser and the exhaust pipe, a part of the vertical stabiliser, the rudder, and the rear part of the fuselage.

The targeted tower was damaged but quickly repaired.

Tuđman Under Attack

One controversial incident during the Yugoslav War was the aerial attack of 7 October 1991, in which the RV i PVO targeted the Banski Dvori in the old, upper city of Zagreb: the seat of the Croatian Government and its President – and that while these were almost visited by the President of the Presidency of the SFRJ, Stipe Mesić, Prime Minister Goran Marković, and Croatian President Tuđman. The sole purpose of the attack was to eliminate the top command and control chain of the Croatian armed forces, which, from the perspective of the JNA, was a reasonable and lucrative target.

At 1447hrs, an air raid warning was issued for Zagreb, and at 1501hrs, Banski Dvori became the target of an air strike, with rockets hitting Dubravkin Put street just a minute later. At that time, Tuđman had finished a meeting regarding the situation on the battlefield in Western Slavonia. In the vicinity, General Anton Tus, the chief of the Croatian Main Staff, and Mladen Vedriš, the chief of the Crisis Staff for Zagreb, were also holding a meeting on the coordination of activities related to the blockade of barracks. One of the topics discussed was the risks of air strikes by the RV i PVO and Tus observed that Zagreb was a large city, and could withstand these, because the air force did not possess the necessary technology to cause a large-scale destruction.[15]

The attack hit home towards the end of that meeting: according to data from the Croatian prosecution, two Galeb-4 aircraft from the 249th Squadron were involved in the mission. One aircraft was armed with four Mk.82 bombs, while the other carried four L-128-04MD launchers with a total of 16 unguided 128mm M74 Munja rockets. Banski Dvori was hit, but the volley of rockets was so dispersed that several nearby buildings were damaged: one member of the Croatian Homeland Defence was killed, and four other people wounded. After the attack, Tuđman's chief of security, Mile Ćuk, could not start the official vehicle from the convoy, so two other vehicles were quickly found to transport them to a shelter in Tuškanac, to the so-called Yellow House, where an information centre was located.

For Croatia, this attack was an important political and propaganda topic, leading to an investigation, but with weak legal grounds. Starting a criminal procedure against the participants in the action was prolonged for decades: it was only in 2016 that the police, military police, and security services obtained and provided to the jurisdiction, 'concrete personal evidence and documentation that are useful for conducting a criminal procedure'. The decision to launch an investigation against six officers of the RV i PVO was made on 12 December 2017, and one year later, in Belgrade, a hearing of six officers was conducted based on a bilateral agreement on mutual legal assistance (five during the same month, and the sixth on 7 October 2020).

The lawsuit for criminal acts against Croatia, including an attempted murder of representatives of the highest state bodies, and war crimes against the civilian population, was filed on 30 December 2020. It was stated that during the investigation, it was determined that the attack was connected to other figures from the highest political and military levels of the former SFRJ. However, a criminal procedure could not be pursued against the officers responsible for ordering the air strikes because they had since passed away, while the evidence against them was deemed insufficient.

According to the Croatian investigation, it was Colonel Slobodan Jeremić, assistant commander of RV i PVO for air support, who informed Major General Ljubomir Bajić, commander of V Corps of RV i PVO, about his plan. The information about the movement of President Tuđman was obtained by counterintelligence officer Čedomir Knežević. Jeremić then flew with a Gazelle helicopter from Bihać to Udbina and established details of the task on which three pilots were to participate: two in Galeb-4s armed with Mk.82 aerial bombs, and one in a Galeb-4 aircraft armed with unguided rockets. The Croatian investigation confirmed that all six individuals involved in the attack were now living in Serbia.[16]

In turn, according to the claims of Major General Bajić, the attack on Banski Dvori was no conspiracy planned in Beograd:

> Simply, at the airport in Bihać, I watched on TV the announcement of the meeting between Tuđman and Mesić in Banski Dvori and made the decision to act. Since the Muslims from Bihać were observing and reporting every take off of our aircraft, I ordered Galeb-4s to take off from Udbina. They came over Zagreb from the north, where no one expected them, they descended to 2,000 metres and fired. One pilot fired rockets, and the other bombed.[17]

The attack on Banski Dvori was the reason for the decision of the Croatians to sever all official links to the SFRJ: this ended a three-month-long 'moratorium' on resolving the country's status according to the Brioni Agreement (see Volume 1 for details).

Velika Buna Barracks

In Velika Buna barracks, located 12–13km from Pleso airbase, the RV i PVO had its 315th ELINT Centre and 5th ELINT Centre, while the JNA maintained warehouses storing weaponry of the Croat TO and various reservist units. Amongst the latter was a self-propelled anti-tank battalion equipped with M18 Hellcats, and a number of US-made M47 Patton tanks of the 205th Armoured Battalion that were in the process of being decommissioned. During the Cold War, the JNA planned to deploy these two units for the defence of Pleso AB, but when the war in Croatia erupted, neither was activated: instead, they relied on reservists from the local population, the majority of whom were Croat. As a result, there were only around 250 officers and other ranks of the JNA in the barracks, and they had to organise a circular defence perimeter, including shelters and trenches, and emplacements for M55 AA guns.

Croatian forces blockaded the Velika Buna barracks for over three weeks. Initially, Zagreb attempted to resolve the situation through negotiations. However, the local commander, Colonel Nikola Ivković, was determined to resist, although his situation was pointless: his unit was principally staffed by reservists with no interest in fighting; it was cut off, surrounded by a numerically superior enemy, and had no chance of successful defence. Nevertheless, all Croat calls for surrender and negotiations were answered with gunfire, which had consequences.[18]

On 6 October 1991, the Croats launched their first attack. For this purpose, they deployed two special police units (Alfa and Roda), parts of the 101st Brigade of the ZNG, the 10th Brigade of the TO, and the Homeland Defence unit from Velika Gorica. The fire was first opened from four 120mm mortars from a battery of the TO sector staff of the South/TO Zagreb. The commander of this unit, recalled that they received an order at 1600hrs that the barracks must fall within 48 hours:

> After receiving the order, we took up a firing position in the village of Kozjača. We started with the artillery preparation at 1800hrs, and after the correction of fire, followed with continuous fire from four weapons. During the firing, the unit was under attack from infantry weapons from nearby cottages

> and barracks. We stopped firing and extracted the equipment and soldiers to a safe area of the forest near Lukavac. During early morning hours and during the night we took a new firing position in the vicinity of the village of Šiljakovina. At 0630hrs (7 October), we started correcting fire on the barracks with two mortars (other armament and personnel were in reserve and secured the firing position) and after that we hit targets in the barracks with bursts [...]. The flow of fire strikes was interrupted by aircraft that flew over us and searched for us throughout the day.

By then, the battery had expended 180 mortar bombs, and four JNA soldiers were killed.[19]

Around 1330hrs, the barracks surrendered. On the Croatian side, the losses included two dead and seven wounded. In the atmosphere of that time, soldiers were not transferred to POW accommodation but were permitted to disarm and change into civilian clothes: whoever wanted to leave the JNA was promptly released. Among the spoils of war were 18 US-made M18 Hellcat self-propelled anti-tank guns: legacy of American military assistance to the JNA from the 1950s. At least as important was the ELINT equipment, forty 20/3 20mm AA guns, and a battery each of 82mm and 120mm mortars. The presence of a large number of captured soldiers was also a guarantee that there would be no counter-action by the RV i PVO, but a day later, on 8 October, a pair of aircraft did strike the Velika Buna barracks, causing a fire in the ammunition depot. Fortunately for the Croats, by then all the armament, equipment and ammunition had already been evacuated.[20]

During the night of 7 to 8 October 1991, Croatian forces in Zagreb were on high alert, prepared for an attempt to seize local military installations. However, in most cases, the crisis was resolved through negotiations and, eventually, an agreement was reached for a withdrawal of most of the personnel and equipment. From mid-October, coordination of actions was agreed upon, with a focus on protection against potential attacks from the east, where aircraft from Batajnica AB were expected, according to Croatian analyses. These expectations did not match reality, as no aircraft from that base operated in the Zagreb area, which was outside their tactical radius. From the south and east, attacks from aircraft based in Bihać were anticipated. The plan involved the formation of a defensive curtain, where each of three emerging air defence units equipped with AA guns was to be responsible for a different sector of the city.

- North (Dubrava district): two Bofors L60/40 and two 20/3 AA guns, and three Strela-2M MANPADS
- Centre: three Strela-2M MANPAD teams and six 20/3 AA guns (all drawn from the 1st Guards Brigade of the ZNG); and
- South: 50th Regiment with a total of 14 Bofors 40mm AA guns.[21]

Positioned in the southern outskirts of Zagreb, Pleso AB survived the blockade, although completely encircled. Arguably, the nerves of the RV i PVO personnel deployed there were put to a tough test. In one attempt to help their surrounded comrades, members of the 151st Air Base who were relocated to Bihać and Banja Luka during the summer, collected money for a large shipment of cigarettes that was to be dropped from a Mi-8 by parachute inside the defence perimeter of Pleso airport. A combination of circumstances led to an error in the assessment of the place of dropping the cargo that fell into the hands of Croatian forces.

The Croatian Armed Forces at Velika Buna barracks captured a number of M18 Hellcat tank destroyers armed with 76mm guns which belonged to the anti-tank battalion for the defence of Pleso base against airborne assault. During peacetime, this was a reserve unit, and its equipment was kept at the barracks. After the start of the conflict, the M18s were brought into service and used on 6 and 7 October. However, they were not of significant use to the Croats due to their complex maintenance requirements and old radial aircraft engines, which were prone to fires and consumed a lot of fuel. (Aleksandar Božić)

VOLKHOV MISSILES

According to Yugoslav doctrine, the air defence of large cities relied on the circular deployment of surface-to-air missile sites. From the late 1960s, the defence of Zagreb was organised in the form of a 'ring' of four battalions equipped with Soviet-made S-75M Volkhov (ASCC/NATO codename 'SA-2d Guideline Mod 3') missiles, all subordinated to the 155th Air Defence Brigade. Headquartered and home-based in Kerstinec barracks, 14km south-west of Zagreb, during the first half of 1990 this unit was greatly weakened as about half of its complement was transferred from active to reserve status. It should be kept in mind that, in peacetime, units like the 155th were staffed only by a small core of personnel even when considered active. Moreover, as of June of the same year, its 1st Battalion was at Cerklje AB in Slovenia; the 2nd was at Cerovac, about 10km south-east of Karlovac; the 3rd was in Žažina, outside Sisak; while the 4th was in Stubička Slatina near Zabok. Only the latter two battalions were kept at the 'A' level of combat readiness.

By August 1991, the 1st Battalion was relocated again: this time to an emergency position near Ličko Petrovo Selo, from where it protected Bihać AB. When Croatian forces blockaded JNA barracks in the Zagreb area, the 155th's elements in Kerestinec, Žažina, and Zabok were affected.

Arguably, the position of the 2nd Battalion was not jeopardised as it relied on the village of Cerovac Vukmanićki, where ethnic Serbs were the majority. Moreover, the Croats were not in favour of an adventurous undertaking like assaulting their bases, because they feared the possible consequences of intentional or unintentional damage to the Volkhov missiles and warehouses. The reason was the very aggressive and hazardous TG-02 liquid propellant and AK-20K oxidiser mix (nitric acid) used in S-75 missiles.[22]

The Croatian CBRN Defence unit created a simulation with the estimate that there were approximately 80 missiles, with two tons of dangerous material, in Kerestinec alone. The assessment was that nitric acid vapours would cause high-risk concentrations at a distance of about 5km downwind of the accident site. It was estimated that TG-2 fuel would not burn completely and therefore contaminate the soil and water in a very wide area around Kerestinac. Due to its carcinogenicity, it would leave long-term harmful effects on important agricultural land. As a result, chemical reconnaissance teams were engaged around the barracks, in addition to the infantry in the blockade, which delivered the collected data to the centres of the Toxicological Service. The CBRN Defence report was forwarded to the Croatian Government and the population was informed about the potentially risky situation.[23]

The local Crisis Staff and military commanders in Kerestinec chose a 'soft' approach to solving the problems. On 27 September, the commander of the Croatian 151st Brigade of the ZNG – Adolf Paar – and the local police commander – Ivan Pazer – met with Colonel Slavko Biga, who was the commander of the 155th Regiment. His command was located in a sixteenth-century castle with two cylindrical towers at the corners. During the meeting, he told the Croats that he was just doing his military duty and that he would not surrender the barracks and equipment. He expected to receive orders to relocate the unit to Bosnia. Until then, he emphasised that incidents should be avoided due to the risk posed by the rocket fuel. Paar recalled that Biga guaranteed that he would hand over the barracks undamaged, but only after the unit was relocated. Until that moment, Biga did not want to initiate an attack if left alone. The Croats made an offer to Biga to join their side, but he refused. Eventually, on 28 October, the 151st Brigade of the ZNG received orders to firmly blockade the barracks and deployed three platoons along the three potential withdrawal routes of the unit. On the basis of a broader agreement for the withdrawal of the JNA from the Zagreb area, parts of the 155th Regiment left Kerestinec only on 29 November 1991.[24]

In Zabok, there was not much tension due to the risk posted by the fuel until the withdrawal of the battalion. However, the situation in Sisak was dramatic as the local command of the Croatian forces wanted to quickly capture all the JNA barracks. Željko Ajduković, an ethnic Croat and an officer in the 3rd Battalion, remembers that the unit had 36 officers and NCOs and around 120 soldiers in the summer of 1991. The professionals sensed the pre-war atmosphere and moved their families to Serbia for safety, while also reinforcing the protection of the barracks. Ajduković provided information to the Croatian police during secret meetings in a restaurant and his apartment. He created drawings of the missile and minefield placement, guard positions, and storage areas, along with psychological assessments of his unit's members. In August 1991, the commander of the 3rd Battalion ordered the placement of anti-personnel mines on the outer side of the barbed wire fence around the barracks. Ajduković refused to carry out the order, which raised suspicions among his subordinates about his loyalty to the RV i PVO. Moreover, he mostly stayed alone in his office and kept an assault rifle nearby. Before the end of August, daily explosions started to be heard in the barracks from the region of Banija, where fighting was taking place between Croatian forces and the TO Krajina. This intensified the nervous atmosphere among the soldiers who had been surviving on conserved food rations since July. At the beginning of September, the Croats captured the Barutana ammunition depot outside Sisak, where an engineer battalion was stationed. This raised the expectations for an attack on the 3rd Battalion, but the defence was prepared and determined to fight. At the beginning of September, two ZNG officers arrived in Žažine for negotiations, but both were arrested and later released after a brief detention. During this time, Ajduković was ordered to throw hand grenades at Croatians if they approached the barracks' fence. He went to the battalion's commander, Major Milojica Vukadinović, and informed him that he was leaving. They agreed that if they had to shoot at each other, they would try to miss.

The continuation of the blockade primarily involved psychological pressure on the barracks' occupants. A Croatian officer, Šikić, the commander of the 55th Light Air Defence Battalion of the ZNG, had multiple conversations with Major Vukadinović, who promised him that he would not take any actions against the city of Sisak. Vukadinović explained that he was an officer of the JNA and was not trained to shoot at civilians and towns but to protect the people. Šikić tried to use Vukadinović's emotions to his advantage and, on 22 September

1991, brought a crowd of civilians to the barracks who had fled from villages in Banija due to the TO Krajina's advance. However, his superiors did not approve of this plan. A tacit agreement was reached to maintain peace on both sides, and negotiations were held to prevent a Croatian attack. In return, the Croats were satisfied as the unit remained inactive, and according to Šikić, they saved Sisak from the effects of the Volkhov missiles. Still, for the duration of the blockade, the 1st Company of the 57th Independent Battalion, ZNG, and parts of the parts of the 120th Brigade were tied down around this site.

Pressure was maintained on Vukadinović to hand over the barracks and negotiations were held for several weeks in October and November about the terms of that act. In the meantime, on 20 November, the general agreement on the eviction of the JNA was signed. The 3rd Battalion left the barracks on 23 November with all of its Volkhov missiles and other equipment.[25]

A V-755 missile (version with Soviet air defence designation 20DP) on a SM-90 launcher in position in the vicinity of Bihać. (Milorad Ristić)

For transporting V-755 missiles to the launchers, PR-11BM semi-trailers and ZIL-157KV tractors were used. In the background on the left side, another missile on a launcher can be seen. Typically, SA-2 SAM launchers were located in star-shaped sites, but the 1/155th Regiment was relocated to a provisional position near the Bihać base in the summer of 1991. (Milorad Ristić)

A P-12NP (ASCC/NATO codename 'Spoon Rest B') surveillance radar, which was used by the air defence missile battalion. (Milorad Ristić)

Sisak Radar Site

The town of Sisak, located on a plain 57km southeast of Zagreb, had a strong Croatian nationalist movement and became the primary base from which combat operations in the Banija region were undertaken. During the summer of 1991, the Croats established the 55th Light Air Defence Battalion in Sisak. Its elements comprised a battery of four M55 and eight M55J 20mm AA guns deployed for the protection of the local oil refinery, and 12 Bofors M1A1 40mm AA guns for the protection of the local ironworks. Moreover, the unit was trained for action against ground targets.[26]

Unlike most towns that had strong garrisons, locally based Federal units included only engineers and reserve formations. Eight kilometres east of the town was the Sašina Greda radar site with a Soviet-made P-14 (ASCC/NATO-reporting name 'Tall King') early warning long-range radar, a P-12 ('Spoon Rest') surveillance radar, and a PRV-11 ('Side Net') height-finding radar – all operated by the II Battalion of the 5th Air Surveillance Regiment. The local Croatian forces were particularly insolent, and the first fatal incident occurred before the official order to blockade the barracks. On 9 September, a water tank truck was supposed to come from Pleso to the radar site. The driver and accompanying NCOs were stopped at the entrance to Sisak and were almost shot. They were stripped of their personal weapons and returned to the base. The next day the same vehicle took a detour and in addition to the driver in the cabin was one officer, chief of the quartermaster service of the 5th Regiment. They were stopped and pulled out of the vehicle. Croatian soldiers summarily executed the officer, while the driver was taken as a prisoner of war and released only 20 days later.

The first direct attack by the Croatian 120th Brigade of the ZNG on the radar site was carried out on 15 September 1991. At that moment the II Battalion was down to two officers, two NCOs, and 26 soldiers, who were organised into a circular defence of the command building, the P-12 and the P-14. The first assault was repelled, but the Croats attempted again a day later, this time reinforced by parts of the 57th Battalion and some police. Around 1700hrs, two improvised armoured vehicles manufactured in Sisak on the basis of two GJ-800B artillery tractors, accompanied by around 20 troops, appeared in front of the entrance. Using a megaphone, their commander requested to speak with the commander, Captain 1st Class Zvonko Šoš, and called on the II Battalion to surrender. Šoš entered negotiations but rejected a surrender and requested that the Croats move away, otherwise he would request air support. What the defenders did not know was that meanwhile 36 other Croat soldiers were in the process of infiltrating their position: after crossing a corn field around the time the negotiations began, they used a dyke to approach the perimeter but strictly followed the order not to open fire until negotiations were over.

Nevertheless, the Federals sighted them and, around 1800hrs, as two MiG-21s from Bihać AB appeared overhead, one red and one green signal flare were fired by the troops of the II Battalion, and the jets turned around to attack the Croatian troops. Both of the Croat negotiators – Marijan Celjak, deputy commander of the 57th Battalion of the ZNG and Josip Šikić, commander of the 55th Air Defence Battalion – took cover in the dyke. Šikić recalled: 'After the rocket attack, the aircraft did not return, but shooting began at the base and around it. Bullets and rifle grenades flew in all directions…'.

He came away unscathed, but Celjak was killed by rocket fragments. That said, because the Croats continued their attack, the troops of the II Battalion assessed the results of the air strike as ineffective. Thus, the fighting went on until around 2200hrs, by when Šoš ordered his troops back into concrete shelters and requested additional air support. Throughout the following night, their position remained under constant mortar fire.

Indeed, around midnight, the Croat forces were reinforced by a detachment of special police. These managed to penetrate the defence perimeter and were stopped only around 0100hrs by another rocket attack by two MiG-21s. By now, the ZNG had one killed officer, eight wounded soldiers, and one GJ-800B armoured tractor, armed with an 82mm recoilless gun, was slightly damaged.

Because of the air strikes and mines, the Croats did not launch another attack for the next five days. Then, around 1000hrs on 21 September, two Mi-8s – escorted by a pair of MiG-21s – appeared and recovered the survivors from the base. After destroying all three radars and their support equipment, all the surviving troops embarked undisturbed and were flown out to Bihać AB, which they reached around 1100hrs. Meanwhile, additional MiGs flew several air strikes on the abandoned compound, adding to the damage. Once inside, the Croats found only a few intact AA guns.[27]

MiGs in Action

Over the following two weeks and into early October 1991, fierce battles erupted all over Kordun and Banija, as the Federal forces attempted to advance in a western direction, reach the border with Slovenia and thus cut-off land communications between central and

A flight line of MiG-21bis. The first aircraft is armed with two launchers with a total of eight 128mm rockets and the next two with two launchers for 32 57mm rockets. (Milorad Ristić)

southern Croatia. The RV i PVO flew a number of close air support sorties, the most significant of which was launched on 5 October 1991. Split into four pairs, eight MiG-21s of the Bihać-based 125th Squadron – each armed with two British-made Hunting BL755 cluster bomb units (CBUs) – first flew north at 6,000m altitude, before abruptly descending to low altitude to attack the air defences of Sisak. Once within the target zone, the pilots then deployed entirely new tactics of 'strafing from long range'. As one of them recalled: '...we entered a shallow dive and opened fire to cover a larger area and increase the dispersion of hits. We intended to force the air defence to lie down as we passed'.

After expending a total of 320 rounds of 23mm ammunition, the jets then turned around to deploy their BL755s. Simultaneously, a pair of MiG-21bis deployed PLAB-350 incendiary bombs against targets on the road from Sisak to Bihać. The leader of the pair, Captain Ivan Selak, had his aircraft hit in the left wing by large-calibre AA gun (most likely one of the Bofors), but made a 360-degree turn and attacked the site that had hit him, before returning safely to his home base. Later the same day, Selak was to pilot an Utva-66 (number 51184) piston aircraft on a liaison mission. During the take-off, the aircraft stalled and crashed, and his co-pilot and technical officers were killed: Selak survived with severe burns on his head, back, and hands.[28]

A MiG-21bis from the 125th Squadron in preparation for take-off on a combat mission. (Milorad Ristić)

The Utva-66 liaison aircraft with registration number 51184 was lost in an accident on 5 October 1991, at Bihać. Before the war, this particular aircraft was assigned to the 129th Fighter Aviation Squadron at Pula in Istria. It was transferred to Bihać along with that unit. This photo of the aircraft was taken in March 1991 at Zemunik. (Dragan Veličković)

3
THE MOUNTAINS OF CENTRAL CROATIA

Situated on the border between the Lika region of Croatia, and Bosnia, at the foot of the northern part of Mount Plješevica, was the sprawling Bihać AB. This highly important facility had all of its major installations – except for aprons and runways – constructed underground and was the home base of the 117th Aviation Brigade. This was a large unit comprising three squadrons of MiG-21s, and one flight equipped with Orao and Jastreb reconnaissance aircraft. Since 30 August 1991, it had been subordinated to the headquarters of the 238th Fighter-Bomber Aviation Regiment, home-based at Banja Luka AB. Moreover, contrary to the original plan and the very purpose of Bihać AB, out of concern about possible accidents, all the missions were prepared on the tarmac, in the open, instead of within its extensive underground facilities.

Because the base was constructed near several villages predominantly populated by Croats, its command – the 200th Air Base – took extensive protective measures. It controlled the 200th Light Air Defence Artillery-Missile Regiment (comprising a battery of 40mm Bofors L/70 AA guns, two batteries of 20mm M55A4 AA guns, and a battery of Strela-1M MANPADs; reinforced by a battery of Strela-2M MANPADS), a task force from the 63rd Parachute Brigade, a company of T-55 tanks from the 329th Armoured Brigade, the 166th Anti-Tank Battalion with M18 Hellcats, and various minor ground forces. Amongst others, the paratroopers 'cleared' all the Croat villages nearby, driving their population into Croatia. Still, the communication between the strategically important air base and the HQ of the 5th MD at Slunj was under a constant threat.

Plješevica Radar Station

Long before the war in Croatia, the RV i PVO constructed a radar station at Gola Plješevica, the summit of Mount Plješevica, at an altitude of 1,648 metres above the sea level, and equipped with a Marconi S-654 radar that was operated by I Company, 51st Air Surveillance Battalion.[1] Nominally, this was a good piece of equipment, supposed to be capable of providing all weather coverage over extended periods of time. However, when the fighting erupted, it was undergoing a general overhaul. A temporary solution was found by redeploying a US-made AN/TPS-63 L-band, 2D radar from its station in Kurilovac, outside Zagreb, which was usually operated in support of the air traffic service.[2] This operation was completed on 7 July 1991 and proved easier than expected because the system in question – which also proved excellent in tracking low-flying aircraft and helicopters – was mobile and originally considered a 'gap-filler': it could be disassembled in a matter of 30 minutes and reassembled within 60 minutes.

On the same day, paratroopers of the 63rd Parachute Brigade also escorted another major redeployment: that of a S-600 radar of I Company, 91st Air Surveillance Battalion (including the S-5014B Furnus cabin and its large S-1020 antenna) from Mount Ljubljanski Vrh, in Slovenija, to Plješevica. This system was meant to replace the S-654 that was down for maintenance and its redeployment was completed in two runs on 18 and 24 August, when columns with elements of the radar system, its cabins, generators, and two geodesic radar domes, were driven all the way from Ljubljana to Plješevica, and then installed in their new place, despite extremely complex meteorological conditions and massive maintenance issues. The new radar station became operational on 23 September. The AN/TPS-63 was kept nearby until 8 October, when it was relocated to Mount Kozara, in north-western Bosnia and Herzegovina.

Closer to Bihać AB, at the site coded K-377, the RV i PVO had another radar station. Operated by the 1st Air Surveillance Regiment, this was equipped with an AN/TPS-70 phased array, 3D radar. However, on 13 August 1991, this system was relocated to Serbia.

Bihać Air Base at War

MiGs of the 117th Aviation Brigade flew their first combat sorties on 14 September 1991 – on the first day the Croats imposed a total blockade of the barracks around their country. One of the veteran pilots that flew with the 125th Squadron that day recalled that they were put on alert around midnight and briefed to prepare 12 aircraft: four armed with BL755 CBUs, four with 240mm S-24B unguided rockets, two armed with pods for 128mm Munja unguided rockets, and two with four UB-16-57 pods for 57mm unguided rockets. Additionally, a single MiG-21UM was armed with napalm tanks. Eventually, the unit was tasked with flying only four sorties: two (armed with UB-16-57s) against Croat positions at the Prezid pass, on Mount Velebit, and two (both armed with S-24Bs) against a position near the Paški Bridge.

Table 1: Aircraft of the 117th Aviation Brigade, Bihać AB, Autumn 1991

Type	Serial Number
L-17	17104, 17106, 17107, 17109*, 17110, 17125, 17126, 17129, 17130, 17133, 17161, 17167, 17169, 17170, 17171
L-17K	17201, 17204, 17205, 17206, 17208, 17209, 17210, 17211, 17212*, 17213, 17214, 17226, 17229, 17235, 17405, 17407
L-14	22707, 22724, 22735
L-14i	26101, 26104, 26107, 26108, 26109*, 26111, 26112 (defection to Austria)
L-15M	22865, 22866, 22867, 22868
NL-16	16152, 16153, 16177, 16179, 16180
NL-14	22951, 22953
NL-12	22908, 22909 (did not fly during autumn 1991)
IJ-21	24406, 24407, 24421, 24423, 24425, 24456
N-60	23133, 23172, 23178
*shot down	

The next major operation was planned for 8 October 1991, with the aim of improving the land connection to the HQ of the 5th MD. At 0700hrs, a company of T-55 MBTs, a mechanised platoon mounted on M-60 armoured personnel carriers (APCs), and a Sabotage Detachment of the TO Banija, accompanied by some Serbian militia, moved out. However, due to low clouds and rain, the MiGs were unable to provide close air support. Therefore, the attack was postponed to 1300hrs, by when artillery was available instead. Two MiG-21s appeared overhead only once the weather improved, in the late afternoon. That evening, the task force secured Vaganac: on the next morning, it reached Drežnik Grad, and then continued for Grabovica, where a makeshift Croat police HQ was discovered in the local hotel. No further close air support was requested for this operation.

Above and below: In the battles to clear the wider perimeter around Bihać AB, the task force of the 63rd Parachute Brigade was reinforced with M53/59 AA guns borrowed from ground forces. (Ivan Detiček collection)

A solider of the RV i PVO guards the relay station on the top of Čelopek (k. 526), part of the Bihać base communication system, on the northern slopes of Mount Plješevica. (Milorad Ristić)

On the tarmac with a MiG-21R and MiG-21UM, one of the two pilots is heavily armed with a 7.65mm M84 submachine gun and a 7.65mm M70 pistol at his waist, and he is holding a 7.92mmx57mm M76 semi-automatic marksman rifle in his hand. (Milorad Ristić)

A MiG-21UM armed with unguided rockets is seen taxiing at Bihać near Galeb-2s, which had arrived from Cerklje in Slovenia. (Zoran Milovanović)

Pilots of an IJ-22 Orao from the 353rd Squadron from Mostar moved to bases that were closer to the zone in which they performed dedicated reconnaissance tasks. Serial number 25712 was recorded on 1 November 1991. (Milorad Ristić)

T-55A MBTs and M-60P APCs from the 329th Armoured Brigade on a mission to strengthen the defence of vital infrastructure and the 117th Aviation Brigade, photographed from a Gazelle taking off from Bihać. (Dragan Veličković)

Kordun and Banija

The main battlefields in 1991 included the adjacent regions of Kordun and Banija, located south of Zagreb. In the military-territorial organisation of the JNA, this area was the responsibility of the 5th MD. On the northern edge of Kordun was the city of Karlovac, which was one of the major garrisons of the JNA, housing the 580th Mixed Artillery Brigade (5th MD), a mechanised battalion from the 4th Armoured Brigade (X Corps), and the 8th Proletarian Motorised Brigade (XIII Corps), along with various logistic units, and the Engineer Training Centre. The only unit from the RV i PVO was II Battalion, 155th Air Defence Missile Regiment, mentioned in the previous chapter. In Banija, the main strength of the JNA consisted of the 622nd and 257th Motorised Brigades from the Petrinja garrison, reinforced by a tank battalion from the 51st Mechanised Brigade from Pančevo.

In both cities, Croatian armed forces and police completely surrounded the barracks and attempted to force the garrisons to surrender. Even-larger stocks of weapons and ammunition were blockaded by Croats in the town of Ogulin, between Kordun, Lika, and Gorski Kotar, in the barracks and warehouses Oštarije I and Oštarije II, five kilometres southeast of the town, and another five kilometres further at a technical workshop in the Skradnik I barracks and Skradnik II warehouse.

The task of the air force was to support the defence of endangered units, which was carried out by MiG pilots from Bihać. They experienced misfortune on 18 September 1991 when two MiG-21bis were shot down. Captain 1st Class Zlatko Nuspahić (aircraft number 17212) and Lieutenant Bili Levanić from the 125th Squadron took-off for a ground attack in the Petrinja area. The target were the Croatian forces near the village of Brest Pokupski. They conducted two attacks from low altitude. During the third attack run, the

In the defence of Bihać AB, paratroopers had time to practice shooting with various weapons, including this Thompson submachine gun, which originated from American donations in the 1950s. In the RV i PVO, they were used as personal weapons in logistic units, and after transitioning to the M70 family of assault rifles, they were stored in reserve warehouses. (Boško Čeliković collection)

wingman lost sight of the leader. He descended, pressed home his attack and – just before pulling up – observed an explosion on the ground from the direction of the target. Realising it was the crash of his leader's jet, the wingman was startled to figure out that he saw no parachute. Only later on did it become known that the Croat forces saw the pilot ejecting: he was fired upon by multiple infantry weapons while still under the parachute. Croatian forces found the pilot about 100 metres from the wreckage near the Petrinja water supply building. Next to him was an open first aid kit. It remains unclear whether the aircraft was hit, or, more likely, the pilot pulled up before ejecting at a low altitude.

On the same day, four MiG-21bis from the 124th Squadron were tasked with engaging Croatian forces blockading the Oštarije warehouse. The flights separated before the target, and the pairs acted according to an earlier agreement, with the front pair attacking targets south of the warehouse and the second pair to the east and north. The wingman in the rear pair was Captain Goran Mandić (aircraft number 17109). He attacked with Munja rockets from an altitude of 300 metres. At the moment of firing, Mandić felt a slight vibration in the aircraft and noticed a change in the engine sound. After releasing the firing button, he felt as if he continued launching the rockets. Therefore, he pressed the button once more, but no pods were aboard anymore. Pulling out of the attack at an altitude of about 150 metres and rolling out into horizontal flight, he could hear noise from a large flame becoming louder, and thus reduced the throttle. At that point in time he realised that he had been hit, reportedly by a 12.7mm/.50-cal Browning M2HB heavy machine gun. Due to the fire on the aircraft, Mandić had to eject, but as he grabbed the handles he passed low over a hill and noticed a number of scattered private homes in front. Therefore, he decided to continue flying and ejected only when the speed dropped to less than 400km/h and the altitude to 50 metres. He freed himself from the parachute and fled in the direction of the plane crash and tried to hide as shots were fired from all sides. At that moment, above the pilot, a MiG-21bis flew by. He waved to attract attention, especially since the Croats did not shoot while the plane circled. Above him, Mandić saw the jet of his leader, Captain 1st Class Predrag Lovrić, who, as soon as he heard the message that his colleague was hit, quickly aligned his MiG along the path that the downed aircraft took and engaged with the 23mm GSh-23 gun. He saw the mushroom cloud of smoke and continued circling for 10–12 minutes, trying to spot his downed colleague. Due to a lack of fuel, he had to return to base. At that moment, the Croats opened fire again on Mandić. He switched position and tried to hide in another place, but defenders of the village found him after half an hour. They handed him over to the police, and Mandić was a POW until an exchange on 25 November 1991.[3]

Federal Advance to the River Kupa

According to the directive of the ŠVK on lifting the blockade of barracks and establishing effective control over Kordun and Banija, it was the primary task of the JNA units in Kordun and Banija to break through to the outskirts of Zagreb, as described in Chapter 2. For this purpose, the JNA first planned to establish a narrow corridor from Kordun to the north-eastern part of Lika. This was to be accomplished by light forces from the 6th Partisan Brigade, reinforced by a tank company from the 329th Armoured Brigade, operated as the left flank of Operative Group 1 (OG-1). West of OG-1, OG-5 was to break through along the route Plitvice–Rakovica–Slunj–Tušilović, and secure Drežnik Grad and Slunj. Finally, the two groups were – supported by air force and artillery – to establish contact with the besieged 169th Motorised Brigade and in a joint operation lift the blockade of the barracks in Karlovac. However, the Croat forces proved far more resilient than expected, and losses were higher, and OG-1 eventually limited its activity to occupying areas primarily populated by the Serbian majority.

This was particularly ironic considering the RV i PVO achieved quite a feat in this area: On 4 October 1991, MiG-21s from Bihać AB attacked a battalion of the 110th Brigade of the ZNG that was

A MiG-21bis pilot from the 125th Squadron before taking off on a mission for which 128mm rocket launchers are suspended under the wings. (Milorad Ristić)

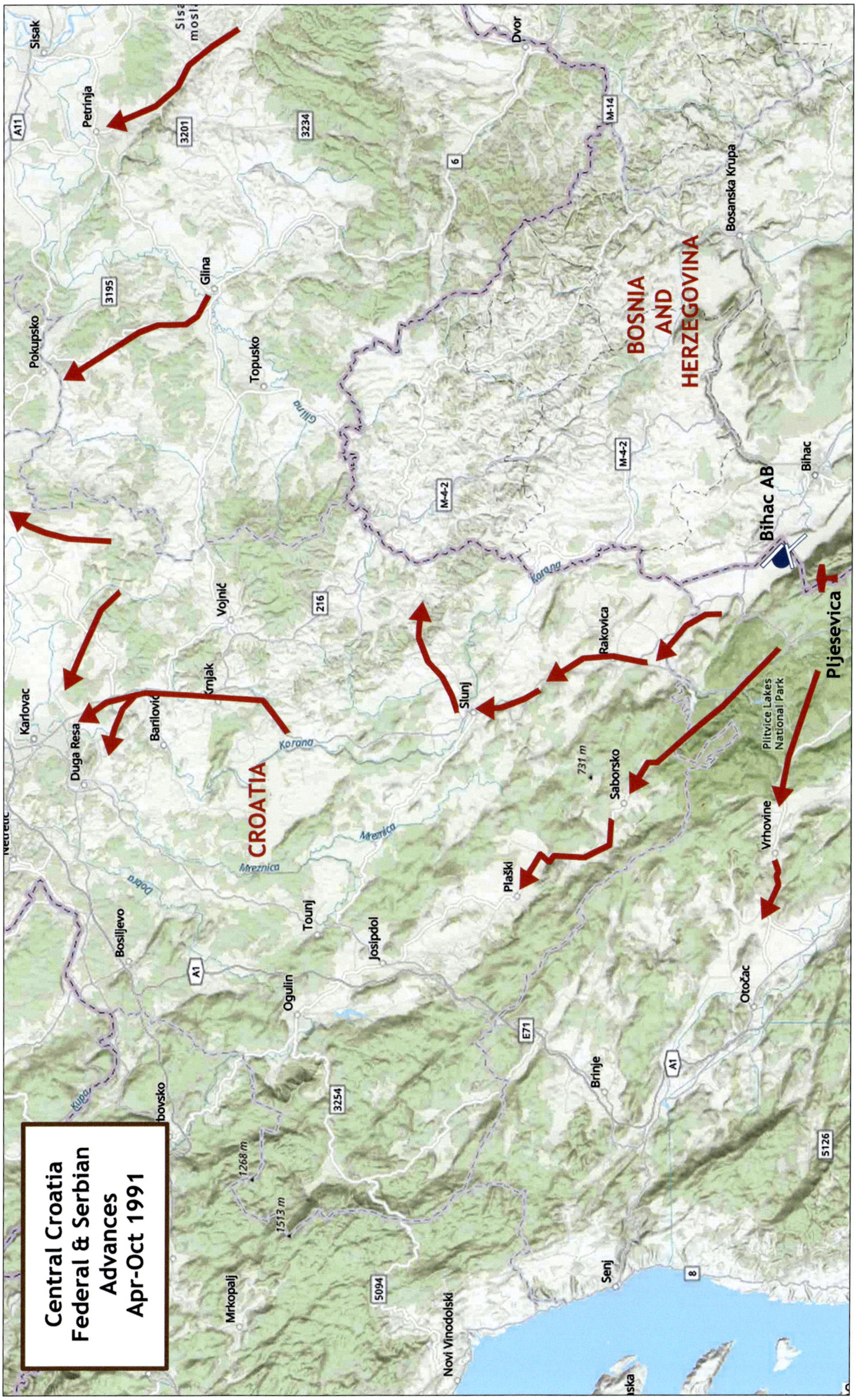

(Map by Tom Cooper)

controlling the Slunjska Brda hills, including a section of the road from Karlovac to Slunj. Following the loss of three soldiers killed and 10 wounded (one of whom subsequently died), the command of that unit assessed its positions as being untenable and withdrew back towards Karlovac, enabling the left flank of OG-1 and the right of OG-5 to launch a major advance on the city. Eventually, the Federal troops were stopped only in the course of bitter house-to-house fighting for Turanj – a village overlooking the confluence of the rivers Mreznica and Korana, less than three kilometres south of Karlovac.

MiGs were less effective while attacking Slunj: this predominantly Croat-populated town had to be isolated in set-apiece advance by OG-5. Initial advances on 9 and 10 October achieved a breakthrough and resulted in encirclement of the town, but Slunj remained under firm Croat control until 16,000 locals fled to Bosnia and Herzegovina. The defenders fought on and were overpowered only in the course of bitter fighting between 16 and 27 November 1991. While this was a major success of the JNA, it was accompanied by widespread atrocities against Croatian civilians that remained behind.

North-east of Karlovac, the 622nd Motorised Brigade was tasked with seizing the roads connecting Petrinja with Sisak, Brest, and the villages Gora, Viduševac and Nebojan. The Croats rushed to construct field fortifications and held out through late September and into early October – also thanks to a pontoon bridge over the River Kupa, constructed between the villages of Letovanić and Nebojan. On 6 October 1991, the 125th Squadron was tasked with destroying this vital communication: unusually enough, the unit sent just one MiG-21 on this mission, armed with four UB-16-57 pods for 57mm unguided rockets, and 180 rounds for its 23mm internal gun.

Despite bitter Croat resistance, on 8 October OG-1 managed to cross the River Kupa east of Karlovac near the village of Jamnička Kiselica, thus also reaching a point only 33km away from the surrounded barracks in the Zagreb area and only 26km from the 4th Armoured Brigade in Jastrebarsko. However, at that point in time, the EC initiated negotiations for the withdrawal of remaining JNA forces from the isolated garrisons. The Croatian armed forces exploited this opportunity to prepare a counteroffensive in which they made extensive use of arms and equipment recently captured from military bases they had managed to overrun. On 28 October, following a strong artillery preparation, they counter-crossed the River Kupa along the road from Pokupsko to Vidoševac. The JNA was thus forced to stop, reroute some of its units and counterattack three days later: this forced the Croats back to the western side of the Kupa. The local Serbian TO units even managed to cross the river over a bridge sabotaged by the Croats during their withdrawal. However, that was about the maximum either side could achieve at the time: the frontlines in Kordun and Banija were subsequently 'frozen' – and remained in their place until August 1995.[4]

DEFECTION OF A MIG-21R

On 25 October 1991, Rudolf Perešin, pilot of the MiG-21R number 26112, took-off from Bihać AB for a reconnaissance mission aimed to cover the withdrawal of the 1st Armoured Brigade from the Vrhnika barracks near Ljubljana, in Slovenija, to the port of Koper. While approaching the latter, he suddenly descended to low altitude, activated the afterburner and turned towards Ljubljana. From there, Perešin continued north – towards Austria – using local hills to hide from the radars of the RV i PVO. Once he approached the international border, the pilot climbed higher to better orientate. At that moment, he was picked up by the radars of the Austrian Golden Haube aerial surveillance system and two Saab J105OËs of the *Luftstreikräfte* (Austrian Air Force) were redirected from a training sortie over Aigen im Ennstal to intercept. Rather unsurprisingly, the subsonic jet trainers never had a chance to catchup with the much faster MiG, which, at around 0958hrs landed at Klagenfurt-Annabichl Airport.

While his MiG was impounded, Perešin was left to return to Croatia where he received not only a hero's welcome but promptly enlisted in the nascent air force. He continued serving for five years longer: on 2 May 1995, Perešin was killed during a combat sortie in the final Croat counteroffensive that ended the war in that country.

Initially, his MiG-21R – number 26112 – was regularly maintained by ground crews of the RV i PVO periodically sent to Austria, until gradually forgotten. The Austrians carefully preserved the MiG and in 2019 handed it over to the Croatian Ministry of Defence in exchange for one of its disused MiG-21bis.

MiG-21R serial number 26112, is seen here taxiing for a mission flown on 7 September 1991. On 25 October, pilot Rudolf Perešin, defected to Austria while flying this aircraft. (Dragan Veličković)

XIII Corps JNA

In the last pre-war reorganisation plan of the JNA, XIII Corps was deployed in the city (and port) of Rijeka, in the Gorski Kotar region to Karlovac, most of Lika, and all the way to Bihać in north-western Bosnia. This plan was never fulfilled and the war caught the corps in the state of transition. As a consequence, military bases in these areas were occupied by a mix of units from the XIII Corps (Rijeka) and the X Corps (Zagreb), the headquarters of both of which were blockaded. Moreover, in August 1991, the 13th Proletarian Motorised Brigade was evacuated form Ilirska Bistrica in Slovenija to Serbia, while the 25th Motorised Brigade was withdrawn from the Istra Peninsula and the Gorski Kotar region to Bihać: both were subsequently subordinated to X Corps. This left the JNA in the Lika region precariously short of both senior commanders and major units.

Except for MiG-21s from Bihać AB, the RV i PVO had only Galeb-2 and Galeb-4s of the 105th Fighter-Bomber Aviation Regiment based at Udbina AB available. Their primary task was close air support. However, they proved unable to save the 236th Motorised Brigade blockaded within its barracks in the town of Gospić. The largest garrison there – the Kaniža barracks and warehouse – surrendered on 18 September 1991: not only 70 officers and 220 other ranks, but

Aircraft from the base at Udbina were mainly engaged in combat missions in the Lika region. Seen here are Galeb-4s from 249th Squadron on the tarmac in the flight line, armed and ready to for take-off on combat missions. (Milorad Ristić)

At Udbina Airport, on 28 October, Galeb-2 aircraft number 23199 from the 251st Squadron was armed for a combat mission. Two pilots were taxiing towards the PSS when a vehicle with an engine starter collided with the aircraft. Due to the impact, two unguided HVAR rockets fell from the underwing pylons onto the asphalt. The damage to the aircraft was extensive; the right wing was broken, and the left landing gear leg was deformed. The rear part of the fuselage of this aircraft was used to repair Galeb-2 number 24265, which was hit in the tail with a Strela-2M missile on 8 November. (Milorad Ristić)

also six T-55A tanks, seven M-60s, a battery of 105mm howitzers, 76mm M-42 guns, 24 120mm mortars, 12 82mm mortars, eight M55 guns, 12 9M14 Malyutka (ASCC/NATO-reporting name 'AT-3 Sagger') anti-tank guided missiles (ATGMs), and eight Strela-2M MANPADS thus fell into Croat hands. Encouraged by this success, the Croatians launched a local counteroffensive and liberated the villages of Lički Ribnik and Bilaj, both of which had predominantly Croat populations. They were stopped only while trying to seize the village of Medak, which remained under Serbian control.

Nevertheless, jets from Udbina flew daily. Most of the time, Galeb-4s were armed with 57mm and 128mm unguided rockets, but sometimes also with Mk.82 bombs. Galeb-2s were usually armed with two High Velocity Aircraft Rockets (HVARs) and two PLAB-150 napalm bombs, or two HVARs and two FAB-100 bombs, or CBUs containing 16kg mortar bombs.

On 20 September 1991, during a mission against Croat positions near the village of Žabica, Galeb-4 number 23728 from the 249th Squadron was hit by a Strela-2M missile while underway just 50–100 metres above the ground. Its pilot, Lieutenant Zoran Katanić, ejected as the jet was down to 40–50 metres and he landed safely under a parachute outside Brinje (then under the control of the JNA), and was picked up by a Mi-8 helicopter about 15 minutes later.

On a combat mission with Galeb-2 number 23265, Lieutenant Pavel Marčok from the 251st squadron was hit by a Strela-2M. The pilot returned the damaged plane to Udbina airport, although the rear part of the fuselage and the exhaust pipe were destroyed and the exhaust cone of the engine was badly damaged. (Aleksandar Radić collection)

A GALEB-4 THAT SURVIVED A HIT

On 24 September, Croatian forces from Gospić attempted to break through via Medak to Lovinac, just 20 kilometres from Udbina AB. The task of four Galeb-4 aircraft from the 249th Squadron was to engage a column of tanks and combat vehicles. The last pilot in the second pair was Lieutenant Branislav Ivanovski in aircraft 23733, which was armed with four launchers for unguided 57mm rockets. After rocketing the Croatian forces' column, he began pulling up at a speed of 720km/h and immediately initiated a combat turn. He felt a strong impact from a missile hit. Ivanovski recalled:

> The accelerometer needle shot up to over 11. The aircraft was in a strange position, and I first returned it to level flight and checked if it was on fire. Someone over the radio said "You're on fire, eject!" but it wasn't my colleagues. I checked the parameters – speed 350km/h, power nine-five, and temperature 400. The aircraft was very heavy on the controls. I reported that I had been hit and was returning. My brain was working at 200km an hour; I noticed changes in the parameters and tried to cross their territory back to our forces. A short flight, less than ten minutes to Udbina, and I lowered the landing gear. It was the nicest landing of my life – even if I had landed on eggs, they wouldn't have broken. On the runway, the engine was smoking, the hydraulics failed, everything failed, and the aircraft stopped halfway down the runway. I taxied off, got out of the aircraft, and walked like a robot, and only then did I feel shivers.

The rear part of the fuselage of aircraft 23733 was replaced, and it was transferred to Belgrade to a museum where it is the only exhibited item from the collection related to the war fought in 1991 and 1992.

The primary task for the 127th Fighter Aviation Squadron, home-based at Batajnica AB and equipped with 14 MiG-29 and two MiG-29UBs acquired in 1987–1988, was standing Quick Reaction Alert (QRA) for air defence purposes. Usually, two aircraft were kept ready to take-off within five minutes of alert, 24 hours a day. During the fighting in Croatia in late 1991, MiG-29s mainly flew combat air patrols along the border with Hungary. If tasked for ground attacks, they were armed with two, sometimes four, B-8M1 pods – each for 20 S-8KO unguided 80mm rockets – and two R-60MK (ASCC/NATO reporting name 'AA-8 Aphid') infrared-homing, short-range air-to-air missiles for self-defence. This is a reconstruction of MiG-29 number 18108 as of late summer 1991. (Artwork by Tom Cooper)

As MiG-29s of the 127th Fighter Aviation Squadron were ever more often tasked with ground attacks – usually against targets of high value – so also their armament began to vary. As well as B-8M1 pods, their other primary air-to-ground weapons were KMGU-2 containers each with 96 BKF PTAB-2.5 anti-tank submunitions with HEAT/fragmentation warheads. Each KMGU-2 weighed 340kg when fully loaded. Alternatively, two KMGU-2s were loaded on the inboard underwing pylons, two B-8M1 pods on the centre underwing pylons, and R-60MKs on outboard pylons, shown in this reconstruction of MiG-29 number 18113 as seen in late 1991. (Artwork by Tom Cooper)

Due to the lack of time and money, the second Batajnica-based interceptor unit – the 126th Fighter Aviation Squadron – remained equipped with MiG-21s. Its pilots were primarily tasked with air strikes against Croatian forces in Eastern Slavonia. Usually lasting about 20 minutes, their missions ranged over 120 to 150 kilometres. On 1 October 1991, the pilot of this MiG-21bis-K – serial number 17402 – descended particularly low while trying to hit his target with Munja 128mm unguided rockets. Debris from explosions caused by hits caused severe damage, but the pilot managed to return the jet safely back to base: nevertheless, that was the last sortie flown by 17402, because it proved to be beyond economic repair. The jet is now on display at the Aeronautical Museum of Belgrade. (Artwork by Tom Cooper)

As of the summer of 1991, both the 352nd Reconnaissance Aviation Squadron of the 117th Fighter Aviation brigade at Bihać AB, and the 204th Fighter Aviation Regiment at Batajnica AB, still had small numbers of old MiG-21PFMs in operational service. The former operated serial numbers 22707 (shown here, manufactured in 1967 with construction number 5713), 22724, and 22735, while assigned to the latter were 22703, 22704, 22705, and 22729. After overhaul at the Zmaj Works, they received an aluminium overall livery, making them slightly lighter in overall appearance than originally. Standard armament included the GP-9 pod for a twin-barrel GSh-23 gun under the centreline and one UB-16-57 pod for 16 unguided 57mm rockets under each wing. (Artwork by Tom Cooper)

While compatible with BL755 CBUs, through August, September and October 1991, MiG-21bis of the RV i PVO flew most of their ground attacks still armed with UB-16-57 pods. The standard configuration included four of these pods, but sometimes two were replaced by larger UB-32-57 pods. This is a reconstruction of MiG-21bis number 17212 (construction number 75083814, delivered in 1980) from the 117th Fighter Aviation brigade, as flown by Captain 1st Class Zlatko Nuspahić on 18 September 1991. While attacking a target in the Petrinja area, the jet crashed, most likely after pulling up too late, killing the pilot. Following this loss, the command of the 117th Brigade ordered all aircraft to be armed with sufficient bombs or rockets for a single attack run only. (Artwork by Tom Cooper)

The 352nd Reconnaissance Aviation Squadron remained the key unit for reconnaissance operations over the territories under the control of the Croatian armed forces. In addition to photoreconnaissance operations, during the war in 1991 its MiG-21Rs also flew dozens of ELINT missions, configured as illustrated here with the R-container under the centreline. Recognisable by large dielectric panels on its side, this comprised SRS-6 and SRS-7M systems for detection, classification and localisation of electromagnetic signals. The R-container also had a single A-39 camera for filming in the direction of flight along the route, for precise determination of position of the aircraft in relation to detected targets. For nocturnal operations, they could also carry SAB-100MN flare bombs acquired from Poland between 1986 and 1990. (Artwork by Tom Cooper)

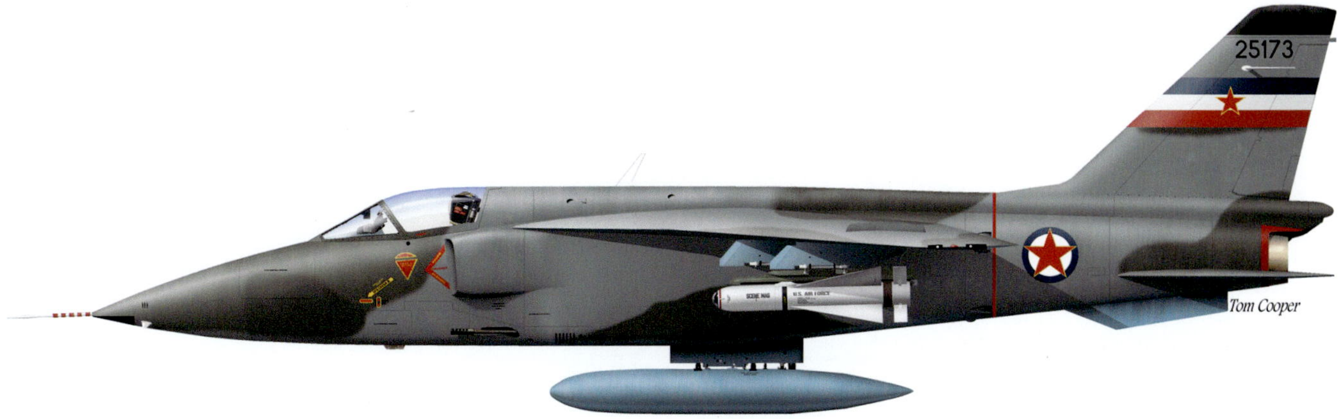

In 1983 – two years before the start of serial production of the J-22 Orao – Yugoslavia acquired 215 AGM-65B Maverick electro-optically-guided air-to-ground missiles from the USA. A total of 15 J-22s were adapted for their deployment: two such jets drawn from the 241st Fighter-Bomber Squadron (numbers 25172 and 25173, shown here), were assigned to the Banja Luka-based 238th Fighter-Bomber Squadron for operations over Croatia. Officially returned to their original unit on 10 October 1991, they actually remained with the 238th Squadron until May 1992, when the Federal armed forces withdrew from Bosnia and Herzegovina, and both were handed over to the Bosnian Serbs. (Artwork by Tom Cooper)

In August 1991, the 238th Fighter-Bomber Aviation Regiment was established at Banja Luka AB. Originally, it included a squadron of seven J-22s from the first production series, manufactured in 1985–1986, all of which lacked afterburners. In October, it was reinforced by two afterburner-equipped examples from the final production batch, including the J-22 serial number 25201. The aircraft here is shown in one of that type's heaviest configurations: armed with four British-made, Hunting BL755 cluster bomb units. A month later, this Orao was one of the first to receive the self-defence system including a pair of flare dispensers attached to the bottom of the rear fuselage. (Artwork by Tom Cooper)

The NJ-22 serial number 25508 was one of several Orao two-seat conversion trainers with operational capability assigned to the Titograd-based 242nd Fighter-Bomber Squadron. From 29 August to 21 September 1991, a detachment of this unit was forward deployed at Tuzla AB, for operations over Eastern Slavonia. On 17 September 1991, commander of the 172nd Regiment, Lieutenant Colonel Muše Begić took off as a leader of a pair of Oraos to conduct a strike on a target in the Đakovo area. While pulling up from his attack with L-57-16- and L-128-4 pods, 25508 was hit by a single Strela-2M. Begić ejected safely from an altitude of 400 metres and was subsequently captured. (Artwork by Goran Sudar)

The Batajnica-based 252nd Fighter-Bomber Aviation Squadron had seven Galeb-4s in service as of summer 1991. Three of these belonged to the pre-production batch with a conventional, fixed horizontal tailfin: these were the first prototype (serial 23004), 23603 (illustrated here), and 23606. The aircraft were primarily deployed for target-towing purposes, with the second seat usually occupied by a technician responsible for handling the towed target. As of 17 September 1991, 23603 was one of few still wearing the full peacetime insignia, including the large tactical number on the nose, applied in white. While piloted by Captain 1st Class Zoran Marjanović in a strike in the Osijek area, and following release of four Mk.82K bombs (US-made Mk.82s equipped with Mk.12 Snakeye retarding fins), it was hit by a Strela-2M missile that knocked out the engine. Marjanović ejected safely and was subsequently captured. (Artwork by Tom Cooper)

As of summer of 1991, Galeb-4 serial number 23647 was one of the most-flown jets of the 252nd Squadron: between early September and late November it was flown in 41 combat sorties, all over Eastern Slavonia. The aircraft is shown armed with a pod for the GŠ-23L (YU) gun under the centreline, and four L-128-04MD launchers, each for four M74 Munja 128mm unguided rockets. The latter were based on L-57-16MD pods for 16 unguided 57mm rockets. Together with rockets for them, these pods were developed from the design of the Soviet-made UB-16-57 pods; the rockets were produced in Krušik, and the pods in Soko Mostar. Such pods were in service on Orao, Galeb, and other aircraft and saw widespread deployment during the fighting of 1991. (Artwork by Tom Cooper)

In the summer of 1991, the Zemunik-based 249th Fighter-Bomber Squadron redeployed to Udbina AB, assumed combat tasks and its pilots applied the cobra emblem on the nose of their aircraft. One of the Galeb-4s assigned to the squadron (all recently manufactured N-62s) was serial number 23733 (construction number 065, manufactured in 1989). On 24 September 1991, it was flown by Lieutenant Branislav Ivanvovski as the Number 4 in a formation that attacked a Croat military column in the Medak area. While pulling up, Ivanvovski's jet was hit by a Strela-2M MANPAD: although the damage caused the aircraft to become extremely hard on the controls, the pilot managed to return it for a safe emergency landing at Udbina AB. The aircraft was repaired through the installation of a factory-fresh rear fuselage (still in its light green primer). Through the 1990s, this jet served with the 252nd, 229th, and 242nd Squadrons, while in 1999 its badly damaged fin was put on display at the Aviation Museum of Belgrade. (Artwork by Tom Cooper)

Developed in the 1950s, and manufactured in series from 1965 until 1985, the SOKO Galeb-2 (colloquially 'G-2') mainly served as a jet trainer at the Air Force Academy, and as a continuation trainer and squadron-hack with a few operational units. In 1991, Galeb-2s were heavily deployed to fly ground attack missions in Croatia. This Galeb-2, serial number 23199, was assigned to the Udbina-based 251st Fighter-Bomber Squadron: on 28 October 1991, it was involved in a collision with a ground vehicle in which its right wing was badly damaged. Subsequently, its rear fuselage was used to repair Galeb-2 serial number 24265, badly damaged by a Strela-2M MANPAD on 8 November 1991. The jet is shown armed with an L-57-16 pod for 57mm unguided rockets – the Yugoslav version of the Soviet-designed UB-16-57 – and HVAR 127mm/5-inch unguided rockets. (Artwork by Tom Cooper)

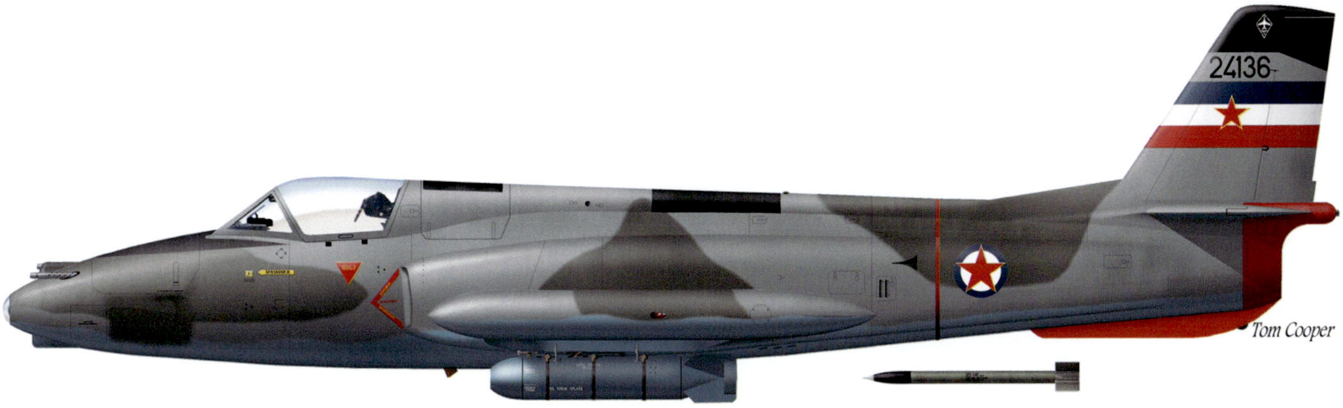

The J-21 Jastreb was the single-seat attack derivative of the Galeb-2. Apart from the single cockpit, the primary other difference was the installation of three Browning 12.7mm/.50-cal machine guns in the nose. Although slated for replacement by the Galeb-4 and J-22 Orao, the type was still in widespread service as of 1991 – including, amongst others, with the Batajnica-based 262nd Fighter-Bomber Squadron. Early on 16 September 1991, two Jastrebs from this unit were tasked with armed reconnaissance of a border post outside Donji Miholjac when the jet piloted by Captain Dragoslav Ranđelović was first hit by a single 7.62mm bullet and then a Strela-2M MANPAD. Ranđelović ejected safely and was captured. The jet is shown armed with a KPT-100 CBU installed on the inboard underwing pylon. This was a relatively simple weapon containing eight 16kg mortar bombs. Shown inset is a single HVAR 127mm/5-inch unguided rocket, as supplied to Yugoslavia in huge numbers by the USA during the 1950s. (Artwork by Tom Cooper)

The NJ-21 was the two-seat variant of the J-21 Jastreb that retained its slightly longer nose in comparison to the Galeb-2, but was armed with only two internally installed 12.7mm/.50-cal machine guns. Built in 1977, as of 1991 serial number 23511 was serving with the 237th Fighter-Bomber Squadron at Cerklje AB. Following evacuation from Slovenia, this unit was disbanded and some of its aircraft and personnel reassigned to the Banja Luka-based 238th Fighter-Bomber Squadron. The jet is shown with its tactical number overpainted, and in a typical weapons configuration from the period of September–October 1991, armed with an FAB-250 M72 bomb (Yugoslav copy of the Soviet-designed FAB-250M-54), and HVAR 127mm/5-inch unguided rockets. (Artwork by Tom Cooper)

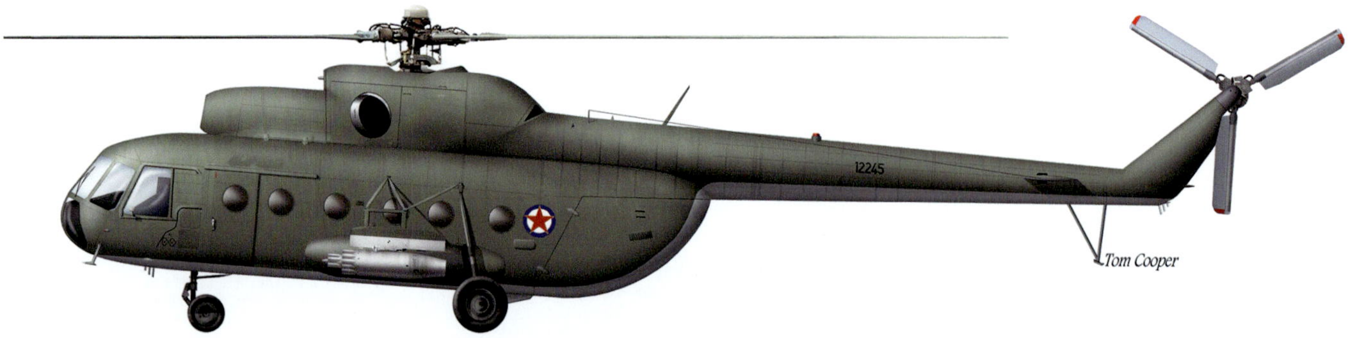

The venerable Mil Mi-8MT continued serving as the primary assault and transport helicopter of the RV i PVO throughout the war in Croatia in 1991, and the type played a prominent role in the evacuation of several minor garrisons, as well as in keeping others resupplied. Mi-8s of the Batajnica-based 890th Squadron became involved in safeguarding, and later evacuating, the crucial communication node at the peak of the Dilj Gora, outside Slavonski Brod. On 4 October 1991, during the evacuation of this small garrison, while underway from Slavonski Brod and heading south, the Mi-8MT serial number 12245 passed low over the position of the 3rd Company, I Battalion, 108th Brigade, ZNG, and was shot down by small-arms fire. The white serial applied atop of the fuselage might have been over-painted by the time. (Artwork by Tom Cooper)

In the summer of 1991, the government in Belgrade assigned two Aérospatiale/SOKO SA.341 Gazelle helicopters of the 890th Transport Helicopter Squadron to the European Community Monitoring Mission (ECMM) – the first foreign mission active during the war in Yugoslavia, established on the basis of the Brioni Agreement, singed on 7 July 1991. To make them easier to recognise by the ground forces of all the involved parties, both helicopters – serial numbers 12893 (shown here) and 12894 – had most of their booms painted in white while retaining their national markings and other insignia. Eventually, neither saw any service with the ECMM because of disagreements between that body and the warring parties. Nevertheless, they continued serving in this livery and supported JNA units in Eastern Slavonia and Vojvodina throughout the autumn of 1991. (Artwork by Tom Cooper)

Two Sud Aviation/Aérospatiale SE.3160 Alouette IIIs from the Liaison Aviation Squadron – a unit directly subordinated to the Command of the I Corps RV i PVO – were regularly deployed for the transport of senior officers to important conferences and meetings. Despite the fighting, both retained their smart livery in white and blue, as well as high-visibility markings. Throughout the last quarter of 1991 alone, serial number 12151 made no fewer than 367 flights, while the other helicopter of this type – serial number 12152 – made another 89. (Artwork by Luca Canossa)

During the summer and autumn of 1991, the 63rd Parachute Brigade was mobilised and expanded through the infusion of reservists. Its detachments were deployed for the defence of air bases at Cerklje, Pleso, Pula, Bihać, and Mostar, and also conducted numerous assaults to clear nearby Croat positions. Furthermore, the brigade established several combat search and rescue teams, responsible for recovering downed pilots. Paratroopers of the 63rd usually wore camouflage fatigues and leather boots. Their primary firearm was the Zastava M70 assault rifle (as shown here), M72 light machine gun, or the Zastava M76 semi-automatic 7.92x57mm marksman rifle. (Artwork by Renato Dalmaso)

Pilots of the RV i PVO entered the civil war wearing light blue overalls, introduced in the mid-1980s. The only regulation insignia were the service crest worn on the left sleeve, and the rank insignia on a Velcro strip. The principal personal firearm of every officer was the Zastava M70 7.65mm pistol. This Gazelle pilot also armed himself with a Zastava M84 7.65mm submachine gun which was usually acquired privately. Although issued with helmets, helicopter pilots usually flew without them, wearing just their earphones and microphones instead. This pilot completed his uniform with a cap, with a small red star, issued to the anti-terrorist unit of the Ministry of Interior. (Artwork by Renato Dalmaso)

Once the fighting erupted, blue overalls were rapidly replaced by M89 overalls in four colours (dark green, leafy green, brown, and black). These included vests with pockets for carrying Alinco or Motorola portable radio stations, and Zastava M70 pistols. Early on, many MiG pilots also carried Zastava M70 assault rifles with folding stocks, but this practice was soon discontinued. Gloss white helmets were regularly repainted in camouflage colours. G-suits were typically added atop the M89 overalls, and while on the ground and during the winter this combination was often completed by the pilot's brown leather jacket. (Artwork by Renato Dalmaso)

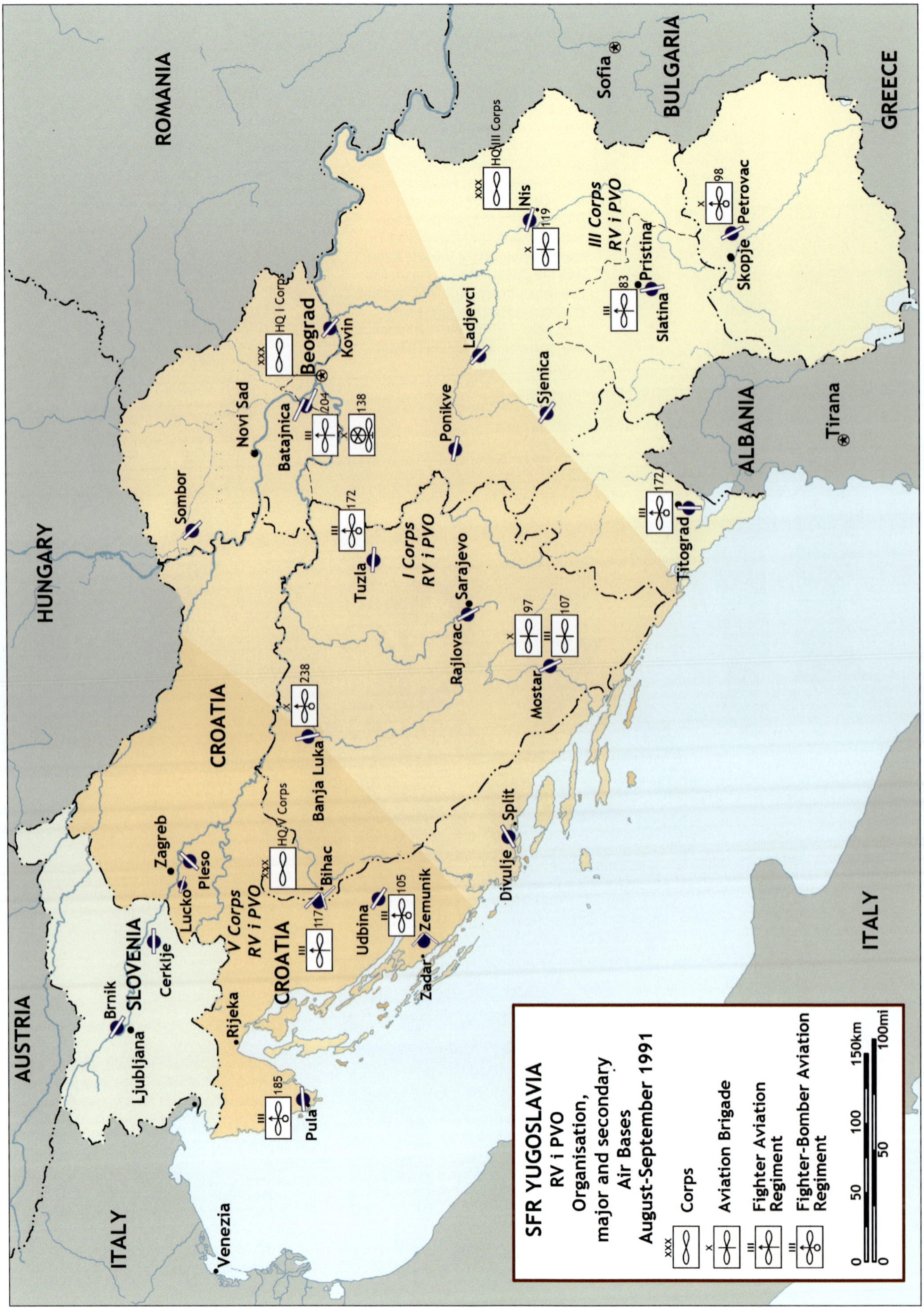

Deployment of major units of the RV i PVO as of August–September 1991. (Map by Tom Cooper)

The damaged fuselage of Galeb-4 number 23733. (Milorad Ristić)

The original tail from Galeb-4 number 23733 is now exhibited at the Aeronautical Museum in Belgrade. (Aleksandar Radić)

Galeb-4 number 23733, shown after the replacement of the rear part of the fuselage at Udbina, continued to fly with 249th Squadron. Later, in the last days of March 1992, it was transferred to Batajnica and 252nd Squadron. During the 1990s, it flew from Golubovci with 229th and 242nd Squadrons, and under an order dated 31 December 1999 it was returned to Batajnica where it was still located at the time this book was written, in late 2024. (Milorad Ristić)

4
WESTERN SLAVONIA

On 12 August 1991 ethnic Serbs from the region of Moslavina, in Western Slavonia, declared an autonomous area and, with support of the local TO, took control over Daruvar, Pakrac and numerous villages in this area. Arguably, there were no JNA garrisons around: the sole Federal unit present was a battalion-sized task force from the 265th Mechanised Brigade, which was deployed in the Okučani area from 14 August (the rest of the 265th was garrisoned in Bjelovar, a town about 80km east of Zagreb, as recounted in Chapter 2).

Three days later, on 17 August, the 329th Armoured Brigade of V Corps from Banja Luka, broke across the bridge over the Sava River into the town of Gradiška and advanced on Okučani. After battles around the village of Nova Varoš, a bridgehead was formed to bring in additional forces from V Corps. In preparation for the battles in Western Slavonia, numerous units from V Corps were mobilised in Bosnia's Krajina. In most places, Serbs were the majority, but with a significant presence of Bosniaks and Croats. During mobilisation, this reflected on recruitment because non-Serb reservists did not show up: in Prijedor, for example, just 40 percent of the 343rd Motorised Brigade's nominal complement was mobilised. In Banja Luka, the 16th Proletarian Motorised Brigade was activated, but remained largely incomplete. Therefore, they were supplemented by two partisan brigades (light infantry), and a motorised battalion from the 84th Motorised Brigade from Bitola in Macedonia. Rounding out this force were the 5th Mixed Artillery Regiment and the 5th Anti-Armour Artillery Brigade. As if aiming to increase the resulting chaos, the HQ of V Corps then declared the 329th Armoured Brigade to be its main striking force – although by then this unit had been chopped apart: its three tank battalions were scattered all over the regions of Kordun, Banija, and Lika, and at least a company was protecting Bihać AB.

The strategic pivot for V Corps and for the battles in Western Slavonia was the garrison in Banja Luka. From mid-August, the local air base hosted Orao and Jastreb aircraft from the 238th Squadron, which was relocated from Slovenia.[1] At the beginning of the offensive in Western Slavonia, that unit had only seven single-seater J-22 Orao aircraft (one of which was soon shot down), three NJ-22 Orao two-seaters (one of which was borrowed), and 10 Jastreb jets.

The equipment of the 111th Aviation Brigade was evacuated from Pleso AB (outside Zagreb) to Batajnica AB by An-26 aircraft, while Mi-8s and Gazelles were temporarily stationed in Bihać. A permanent solution for accommodation was found at the Zalužani barracks, located 10km north of Banja Luka. During the Second World War, that location served as an airfield used by the Croatian Air Force and Luftwaffe for actions against partisans. After the war, in the 1950s Zalužani housed a training unit with Yakovlev fighters and locally-manufactured 213 trainers. After its disbandment in 1956, only aircraft from the local aero club used the grass runway, until Mi-8 helicopters from the 780th Squadron and Gazelles from the 711th Squadron were stationed there in the summer of 1991.[2] The security in the rear, at both Banja Luka airports, was taken over by members of the 474th Air Base, relocated from Cerklje.[3] Of course, the command of V Corps could call upon MiG-21s from Bihać AB.

Table 2: Aircraft of the 238th Fighter-Bomber Aviation Squadron, Autumn 1991

Type	Serial Numbers
J-22	25105, 25111, 25114, 25115, 25116 (damaged in an accident on landing), 25119, 25122, 25123*, 25124, 25153, 25201 25172, 25173 – Oraos from the 241st Squadron were in Banja Luka base from 17 September to 10 October
NJ-22	25503, 25504, 25528 (borrowed from the 242nd Squadron and returned)
J-21	24148, 24160, 24202, 24205, 24209, 24218, 24251, 24258 arrived 24212, 24261
NJ-21	23509, 23511
*shot down	

Table 3: Helicopters of the 712th Anti-Armour Helicopter Squadron, November 1991

Type	Serial Numbers
HN-42M Gama (SA.341H attack version)	12806, 12807, 12812, 12818, 12819, 12820, 12821, 12822, 12824, 12825, 12826, 12828, 12831, 12832, 12835, 12836
HN-45M Gama (SA.342L attack version)	12921, 12922, 12923, 12924
H-42 (SA.341H)	12612, 12665
H-45 (SA.342L)	12877

Table 4: Helicopters of the 78th Transport Helicopter Squadron, November 1991

Type	Serial Numbers
HT-40	12204, 12205, 12211, 12213, 12219, 12222, 12224, 12239, 12244, 12262, 12268, 12305, 12313, 12403, 12405, 12406, 12407

During the night of 15 to 16 September 1991, the task force from the 16th Brigade crossed the Sava River and was introduced into combat actions in the direction of Okučani–Rajići–Novska. They linked up with the task force of the 265th Brigade in the Prašnik forest area. The aviation supported this operation right from the start. Its first task was to locate and destroy a meteorological radar used for military purposes. Two Jastreb aircraft from the 238th Squadron were the first to initiate the attack, and their mission was to designate the target for precise action by two Gama (armed Gazelle) helicopters from the 711th Squadron equipped with Malyutka ATGMs. The pilot who led the pair on that task recalls that at one point, he saw the helicopter hovering just above the Croatian artillery position, and they quickly moved away from that hot spot: 'I have never seen my helicopter move so slowly'.

On 17 September, Major Zoran Tomić took-off from the Banja Luka base for an assignment in the J-22 Orao with the serial number 25123. It was a solo flight, so there were no witnesses from the RV i PVO who could testify to the sequence of events. The subsequent investigation assumed that most likely the jet was shot down by ground fire: Croatian sources state that the plane was hit by a Strela-

2M while underway at low altitude over Novska and crashed near the village of Kozarica. Allegedly, the shooter was from the III Battalion, 1st Guards Brigade of the ZNG.[4]

The plans of the ŠVK for the broader Western Slavonia and northern Croatia were to hold the territory while units blockaded deeper inside Croatia would break through in this direction. With the directive issued by 1st MD on 19 September, the operation by V Corps in Western Slavonia was initiated with the task of transitioning to an 'energetic attack' on the main axis Okučani–Pakrac–Virovitica and the auxiliary axis Okučani–Kutina, with the mission to coordinate with aviation and artillery support and cooperate with the TO. By that time, the plan of the ŠVK and 1st MD for Western Slavonia was expanded: now the intention was to cut-off the retreat route for Croatian forces from east and central Slavonia. The battles in that area escalated prematurely, ahead of the general plan, as local Serbian units entered the war well-organised and imposed their own dynamics.

In the northern part of that area, there was a TO unit – the 28th Partisan Division. At higher new command and control levels, it was expected that the movement of V Corps would relieve pressure from XXXII Corps besieged in northern Croatia, and that the 265th Mechanised Brigade and the 73rd Motorised Brigade would – with air support – break out from the Bjelovar-Grubišno Polje-Daruvar area. However, both brigades surrendered as they lacked personnel to operate necessary equipment.

Meanwhile, parts of V Corps tried to shift the lines to the detriment of the Croats to the west along the highway towards Zagreb, where the 16th Brigade was stationed, and further south, the 12th Brigade. To the north, from Pakrac towards Daruvar, was the 5th Kozara Brigade. On the eastern part of V Corps' zone, the 329th Brigade was engaged in battles towards Nova Gradiška. On 21 September, aircraft from the 238th Squadron received the task of destroying the presumed location of the Croatian headquarters in Nova Gradiška. In the attack, 12 members of the Croatian armed forces and civilians were killed, 50 were wounded, and two military TAM-150T11 cross-country vehicles were destroyed.

From 4 October, offensive actions were launched by the JNA along the Okučani–Pakrac axes. The main participants in these actions were the 343rd Brigade and the I Battalion, 84th Brigade. On the Okučani–Novska–Kutina and Dubica–Jasenovac–Novska axes, the primary forces were the 16th Brigade, 5th Kozara Infantry Brigade, and 11th Partisan Brigade. The 329th Brigade was ordered to cut off Slavonia and support the breakthrough of armoured and mechanised units from the east.

Croatian forces were destabilised by the air attacks. On 4 October, two Orao aircraft took-off, each armed with four SN-3-100 racks, each with three RAB-100 bombs – for a total of 12 100kg bombs. The building of the Defence Secretariat in Novska, where the local military and civilian leadership was located, was directly hit. Nine members of the Croatian forces from the 56th and 62nd ZNG and National Guard Battalions were killed, 23 were wounded, and one civilian died. This caused a breakdown in the command system; part of the command lost contact with units in the field, and some of troops fled all the way to Zagreb. The defence became disorganised, but the JNA did not have intelligence information about this and did not capitalise on the opportunity for a quick advance along the highway in the direction of the Croat capital. By the night between 6 and 7 October, the defence system no longer existed, but the JNA halted its offensive and stopped at the achieved positions. By then, the 16th Brigade had reached the village of Paklenica, and Novska was on the verge of falling.

The air attacks on 4 and 5 October had a significant impact on what Croatian sources describe as 'voluntary withdrawals of defence members' from the town of Jasenovac: this took place on 7 October. A day later, the 11th Brigade entered the undefended town.[5]

After the turbulent first week of October, the JNA halted active operations and showed no interest in supporting local Serbian TO units in the forward areas of Western Slavonia. For the villages that were semi-encircled by Croatians, disaster was inevitable. On 31 October, units of the ZNG launched Operation Otkos-91, the first major counteroffensive in the war, aimed at pushing Serbs out of places in the Bilogora region. Defending these areas were local units of TO and weak JNA forces. On the third day of the battle, on 2 November, Oraos and Jastrebs from the 238th Squadron carried out operations at multiple locations along the front lines and in the depth of the battlefield. Their task was to hinder the advance of Croatian forces and enable the evacuation of the population. The Croats were temporarily halted, but by 4 November they resumed their advance. According to Croatian sources, the actions of the aviation had an effect and bought time for the withdrawal of the TO, but not enough to block the advance of the ZNG.[6]

In his memoirs, Army General Veljko Kadijević later attributed the problems in Western Slavonia to issues in the rear of V Corps. Correspondingly, the reason was the failure to carry out the mobilisation to the extent planned by the ŠVK and, instead of five complete brigades, only forces equivalent to one and a half were actually deployed.

Two Orao aircraft prepared for a combat mission with the classic payload for that aircraft in 1991: two launchers for four 128mm rockets each and two launchers for 12 57mm rockets each. Both aircraft were lost shortly after the photo was taken. In December 1991, the pilot ejected from number 25111 during take-off, due to a technical failure. In an accident on 27 March 1992, the pilot of Orao number 25153 lost his life in a training flight at low altitude. (Miodrag Tarana)

Orao aircraft from the 238th Squadron at Banja Luka base. (Miodrag Tarana)

A Jastreb at Banja Luka armed with a launcher for 57mm rockets and two HVAR rocket with HEAT warheads. (Miodrag Tarana)

The ceremonial parade of the 111th Helicopter Regiment took place in Banja Luka on 21 October, in front of a portrait of Maršal Tito from the time of the Second World War. These were the last acts of the Yugoslav era. The defender of the federation was the commander of the RV i PVO, General Zvonko Jurjević, who formed the unit composed of personnel who had to leave Zagreb due to the war. To his left is Major Srećko Prentović, the regiment's commander. (Mladen Savić)

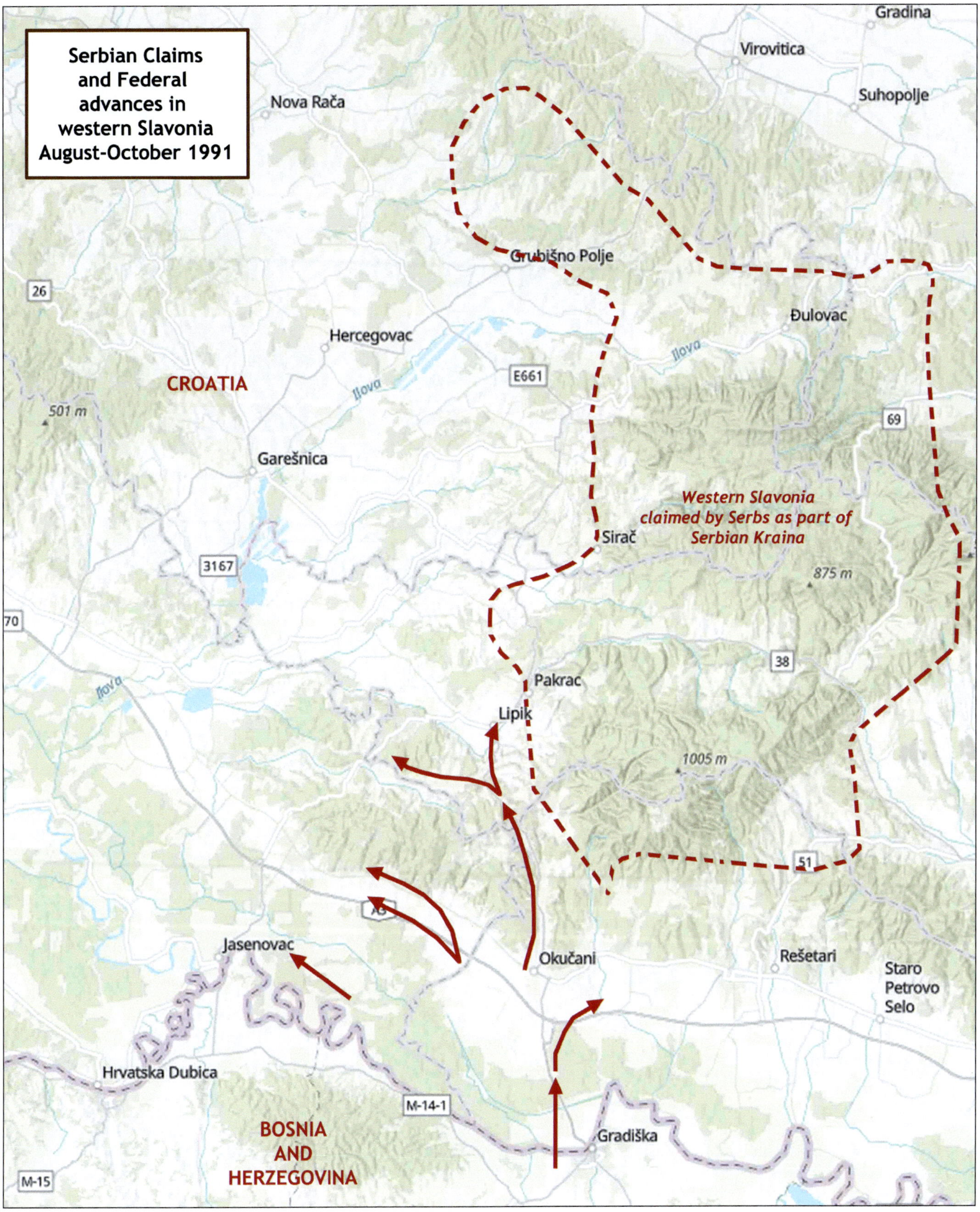

(Map by Tom Cooper)

In the 711th Squadron, the pilots created an emblem with the silhouette of Cerberus. These were transfers that were applied to the pilot suit sleeve using a heated iron. Embroidered chevrons were never made. (Aleksandar Radić)

ARTILLERY RECONNAISSANCE

For the correction of artillery fire, the RV i PVO used Gazelles in the HI-42 Hera version, with an artillery officer on board. A pilot from the 2/896th Squadron, Dušan Maran, recalled a mission of mid-October 1991, when he flew from Rajlovac AB to Zalužane, where he was assigned the task to support the units of V Corps. He landed on a highway extension towards Novska. With the artillery reconnaissance officer on board responsible for monitoring and coordinating the actions of artillery batteries, he then flew towards Croatian positions at low altitude, 'We would pop up above the terrain at about 50 metres height, then move 100 metres to the left, and after a short pause, descend. One day we worked for the artillery towards Novska, the next day towards Jasenovac'.

After a mission in the Lipik area on 14 October, Maran was supposed to return to Rajlovac after landing and refuelling in Zalužani. He recalls flying with a flight technician towards Gradiška, and when crossing the Zagreb–Belgrade highway, due to uncertainty about the location of the forces, 'I went full throttle and flew as low as I could above the Prašnik forest. I heard a sound resembling the impact of pebbles on metal, and I continued low above the tree branches as fast as I could'.

Upon returning to Rajlovac, Maran, together with his colleagues, inspected the Gazelle and saw that it had passed through heavy fire: three rounds damaged two rotor blades, there were 4–5 holes in the tail, and one round passed behind the seat and hit the engine frame. Technicians quickly repaired the damage, and Maran returned to the field with Gazelle 12708 the very next day. He took-off from Zalužani on 17 October:

> I flew at the highest speed I could get out of the machine, at 250–260km/h. A flock of pigeons rose, and the only thing I could do was lower my head and rely on the protection provided by the pilot's helmet. I tightened the control commands to avoid losing control. The cabin cracked. I felt a hit on the cyclic stick and continued on. Air streamed strongly through the cracks in the windshield caused by a collision with a pigeon. I returned to Rajlovac for repair. We found the remains of the pigeon rammed between the seats and the cabin floor.'

5
BATTLE OF VUKOVAR

Much of eastern Croatia – the region known as Slavonija – is situated in the area of the Pannonian Plain: largely flat terrain renowned as well-suited for offensive operations by mechanised units since the times of the Second World War. Indeed, similar conclusions were repeatedly drawn by multiple post-war studies by the JNA which feared a sudden attack into this region in the event of an aggression by the Warsaw Pact. Correspondingly, it deployed many units along the border with Hungary to serve as the first echelon, expected to absorb the initial impact and then, with reliance on the so-called 'bastion' – the mountains of Bosnia and Herzegovina – organise the wartime deployment of the armed forces. In between these locations, the JNA garrisoned multiple mechanised and anti-armour brigades, while motorised brigades were further to the rear.

The rapid collapse of the Warsaw Pact in the late 1980s did not impact the deployment of units. Although Hungary continued hosting Soviet units until mid-1991, planning was modified only in so far that the principal new potential aggressor was the North Atlantic Treaty Organisation (NATO). Therefore, the effective strength of the JNA in the region of eastern Slavonija was in line with the old defence planning. XVII Corps had its command located far from the border – in Tuzla, in north-eastern Bosnia, while its most powerful unit, the 12th Proletarian Mechanised Brigade,[1] was home-based in Osijek, near the border with Hungary.

The basic equipment of the brigade consisted of T-55A MBTs and M-60P/PB APCs. One mechanised battalion from that brigade was, during peacetime, in the garrison of Našice. The engineer battalion was based in Vukovar in a place that in the fall of 1991 became a strong symbol of hatred in the fratricidal war. Further to the rear, 80km from the border, in Đakovo was the 158th Mixed Anti-Tank Brigade, which was supposed to stop the penetration of tanks in the assumed war scenario. Other JNA units of relative strength were the 12th Mixed Artillery Regiment and the 17th Air Defence Artillery Light Regiment, both home-based in Vinkovci. The remaining units of XVII Corps – including three motorised brigades – were all home-based south of the River Sava, in the Posavina region of northern Bosnia and Herzegovina.[2]

East of the 12th Brigade from Osijek, in the northern Serbian province of Vojvodina, were mechanised units from XII Corps: the 36th Mechanised Brigade in Subotica and the 453rd Mechanised Brigade in Sremska Mitrovica. These forces were mobilised and deployed in easternmost Croatia during the summer of 1991, following the outbreak of conflicts between Croats and Serbs, in an attempt to calm inter-ethnic tensions.

After intense clashes between the Croatian police and Serbian Territorial Defence on 2 May 1991, a mechanised battalion from the 453rd Mechanised Brigade (XII Corps) arrived in Vukovar. In August 1991, parts of the 36th Mechanised Brigade were redeployed from Subotica to the Baranja region: a triangular area between the Hungarian border in the north, the Danube River in the east, and the Drava River in the south. Elements of the 51st Mechanised Brigade (XII Corps) took positions on the right bank of the Drava, initially in the villages of Dalj and Erdut, but then moved to the village of Bijelo Brdo – predominantly populated by Serbs, and with a strong presence of their militias based on the local TO structure. This village was located 17km away from Osijek, which soon found itself semi-encircled by as parts of the 12th Mechanised Brigade were redeployed outside the city, at the Bijelo Polje training ground.

With the rest of this territory predominantly populated by Croats, the JNA redeployed the II Mechanised Battalion of the 36th Mechanised Brigade (XII Corps) to protect the main base of XVII Corps in Vinkovci. Moreover, several locally based units were in the field. For example, this included M-53/59 twin 30mm self-propelled AA guns that protected the bridge over the Danube between Ilok in Croatia and Bačka Palanka in Serbia.

Upon the order to blockade the barracks, Croatian forces took actions to isolate JNA bases in Osijek, Vinkovci, Đakovo, and Slavonski Brod. These were places with a Croatian majority in the population, and the Federal forces had no support there except to try to defend their perimeters. The position of the ŠVK was clear: to hold the ground until the arrival of units that were to arrive from Serbia, followed by mobilised reservists. Indeed, following the plan of the ŠVK, the strongest grouping of armoured and mechanised units of the JNA was supposed to engage in Eastern Slavonia, secure the area, and continue rapid actions towards the west to link up with parts of V Corps in Western Slavonia. Together, the two were then to extend further to Zagreb and Varaždin, reaching the border with Slovenia.

Energetic Attack

By the directive of the commander of the 1st MD from 19 September 1991, the JNA's campaign in Slavonia was initiated with the task of launching an 'energetic attack' in the Drava-Sava inter-river area on the main axis, and in Western Slavonia on the secondary axis. The goals were to surround and break the Croatian forces with support of aviation and artillery and collaboration with the Territorial Defence, to lift the blockade on units and military facilities, and to reach the line connecting Našice with Slavonski Brod.

In general, XII Corps held part of the front in the north, and the Srijem/Srem region, while the southern part of the front was the zone of action of the 1st Proletarian Guard Mechanised Division,[3] the Guard Motorised Brigade,[4] and reinforcements, including the 252nd Armoured Brigade (XXXVII Corps). Correspondingly, the task of I Corps and V Corps of the RV i PVO was to provide 'air defence of the main forces from potential reconnaissance and other aviation actions from the areas of Hungary and Austria, and to provide fire support to the ground units'. The emphasis on aviation support was coordinated with the forces of I Corps of the RV i PVO on behalf of XII Corps of the JNA for the Osijek–Našice–Virovitica axis; the 1st Proletarian Guard Mechanised Division on the Vinkovci–Đakovo–Slavonska Požega axis, and a part of forces of V Corps of the RV i PVO along the Okučani–Daruvar–Virovitica axis and the auxiliary Okučani–Kutina axis.

All involved units were to deploy to their starting positions by 2200hrs on 19 September 1991, while the attack was scheduled for two days later. Ground units were explicitly ordered to bypass all the larger populated areas: lifting the blockade of JNA bases in such places was left to the TO.

Every day, pilots from the 252nd Squadron '*Kurjaci sa ušća*' based in Batajnica took-off for combat missions. As described in Volume 1, meanwhile this unit concentrated experienced pilots, almost exclusively of Serbian ethnicity. It also had an unusually large

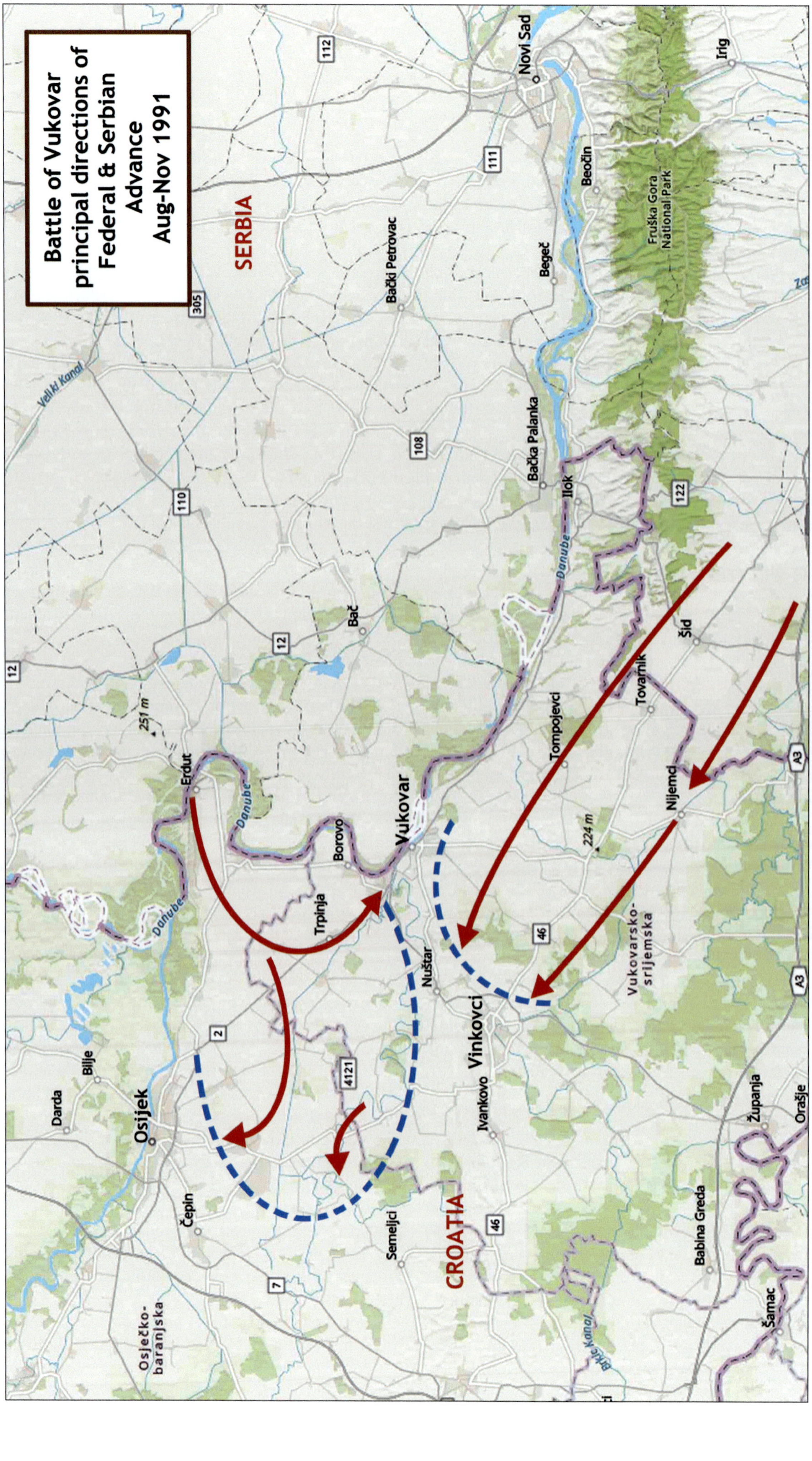

(Map by Tom Cooper)

number of aircraft: instead of the nominal 14, there were no fewer than 47, including 17 Jastrebs, 11 Galeb-2s, seven Galeb-4s, seven Kragujs, and five Utva-66 aircraft. Indeed, it was further reinforced by two IJ-21 Jastrebs (reconnaissance variant), 'borrowed' from the 353rd Squadron based in Lađevci. They were transferred to Batajnica on 18 August and remained there until the beginning of 1992. Due to the need for reconnaissance flights over the flat terrain, aircraft and pilots from the Mostar base occasionally flew such missions too: they operated form Batajnica and Tuzla bases with IJ-21 Orao (353rd Squadron) and J-21 Jastreb (240th Squadron).

Table 5: Aircraft of the 252nd Fighter-Bomber Aviation Squadron, Autumn 1991

Type	Serial Numbers
J-21	24116*, 24122, 24133, 24136*, 24139, 24201, 24208, 24212, 24214, 24220, 24257, 24259, 24261, 24268*, 24272
IJ-21	24410, 24429
N-60	23120, 23173, 23176, 23177, 23179, 23182, 23187, 23204, 23210, 23257, 23266
N-62T	23004, 23603*, 23606
N-62	23630, 23645, 23647, 23734*
J-20	30132, 30135, 30144, 30145, 30148, 30150, 30152
V-51	51124, 51128, 51131, 51133, 51139
*shot down	

Both squadrons from the 204th Regiment – a unit equipped with MiG-29s and MiG-21s – were held at a high readiness rate. Initially at least, the Croats operated no aviation and had only minimal air defences, and thus the RV i PVO enjoyed complete aerial supremacy. Nevertheless, the Supreme Command Staff assessed that there was a high risk of neighbouring countries – especially Hungary – becoming involved. Therefore, part of the interceptor force always stood Quick Reaction Alert for air defence and interceptor purposes. Additionally, both types – the unit had 16 MiG-29s and 30 MiG-21s in operational service – were flown in ground attacks.

Table 6: Aircraft of the 204th Fighter Aviation Regiment, Autumn 1991

Type	Serial Number
L-18	18101-18114
NL-18	18301, 18302
L-17	17127, 17134, 17136, 17151, 17152, 17156*, 17207, 17218, 17220, 17222, 17225, 17227, 17228, 17401, 17402, 17406, 17409, 17410
L-17 (MiG-21IQ)	21168, 21198, 21204
L-14	22703, 22704, 22705, 22729
NL-16	16155, 16175 (15 October reassigned to the 129th Squadron), 16182, 16185
NL-12	22906
V-51	51107, 51247

Reinforcements for the implementation of the directive for the 1st MD arrived from other parts of the state that were not affected by the armed conflict. From Montenegro, parts of the 172nd Regiment were redeployed from Golubovci to Tuzla AB, to provide support in the Eastern Slavonia region. Originally, the entire unit (the 239th Squadron with Galeb-4s, and the 242nd Squadron with Orao fighter-bombers) was redeployed from their home base to Tuzla on 7 July. Later, the Orao aircraft were returned, and from 12–29 August, pilots and technicians from the 239th Squadron were on duty. As the fighting intensified, on 21 September, Galeb-4 aircraft from the 239th Squadron returned to Tuzla. Once the Galeb-4s from the 229th Squadron were withdrawn from Pula AB, the base – originally designed to accommodate just one squadron – was congested.

The focus on combat sorties was on Batajnica's squadrons, and aircraft from Tuzla were assigned to a smaller number of sorties. The branch command considered it crucial to maintain the continuity of training for student pilots at VVA. Therefore, initially, the Orao aircraft, and later on 10 October, the Galeb-4 aircraft were transferred to Golubovci.

On the same day, 10 October, 10 J-22 and NJ-22 Orao aircraft from the 241st Squadron in Petrovac, Macedonia, landed at the Tuzla base. This detachment remained on duty until 8 December.

Table 7: Aircraft of the 239th Fighter-Bomber Aviation Squadron, Autumn 1991

Type	Serial Numbers
N-62	23650, 23675, 23676, 23677, 23679, 23680, 23681, 23683, 23685, 23689, 23700, 23729, 23730, 23731, 23737, 23741, 23742

Table 8: Aircraft of the 242nd Fighter-Bomber Aviation Squadron, Autumn 1991

Type	Serial Numbers
J-22	25122, 15163, 25166, 25168, 25169, 25170, 25171, 25174, 25175, 25201 (on 26 September handed over to the technical test centre for installation of infrared flares), 25202
NJ-22	25506, 25508*, 25509, 25511, 25512 (returned from being reassigned to the 238th Squadron), 25525, 25526, 25527, 25528, 25529, 25531
NJ-21	25512, 25518
*shot down	

Table 9: Aircraft of the 229th Fighter-Bomber Aviation Squadron, Autumn 1991

Type	Serial Numbers
N-62	23624, 23625, 23626, 23627, 23628, 23629, 23631, 23632, 23635, 23636, 23637, 23638, 23640, 23641, 23642, 23643, 23644

The Gama anti-tank and Mi-8 assault helicopters from the 119th Brigade flew combat missions from Batajnica. The detachment consisted of three Mi-8 helicopters from the 787th Squadron and four Gazelle helicopters from the 712th Squadron.

JRV i PVO in the Battle of Vukovar

Right from the start of the offensive, the JNA lacked the necessary dynamics. Instead, it became bogged down in the battle for the town of Vukovar, which began in early August 1991, when the Croats blockaded the local JNA barracks. Eventually, the showdown for this town turned into a symbol of the war in Yugoslavia, becoming the scene of a major showdown between the JNA, the Serbian TO, and a few Serbian volunteer units, against the nascent Croatian armed forces, paramilitary units, and police. As a consequence, the town was almost completely ruined and the resulting footage attracted widespread attention in the world-wide news.

As of 1991, the most modern and the most potent aircraft in the RV i PVO was the MiG-29, but it was rarely used in combat assignments. During wartime, MiG-29 pilots were on Quick Reaction Alert at their home airport, equipped with air-to-air missiles – including two R-27R1 (ASCC/NATO-reporting name

'AA-10 Alamo') and four R-73E (ASCC/NATO-reporting name 'AA-11 Archer').

When flying ground attacks, they were mostly armed with B-8M1 launchers for 20 S-8KO unguided 80mm rockets or four 240mm S-24B rockets. During one sortie for the destruction of a command post, BetAB-500 concrete-piercing bombs, weighing 477kg, were used. These bombs could penetrate up to one metre of reinforced concrete. Additionally, KMGU munition containers, filled with cassettes each containing 96 PTAB-2.5 submunitions with a weight of 1.85 kg each, were sporadically deployed.

One significant advantage of the MiG-29 in the early stages of the Yugoslav War was its self-protection system against infrared-homing surface-to-air missiles. Each aircraft was equipped with two containers, each containing 30 flares, in contrast to other combat aircraft of the Air Force and Air Defence, which lacked such protection.

One of the pilots recalled a combat mission with MiG-29s that he performed in pairs in complex meteorological conditions:

> I flew to Slavonia through cumulonimbus clouds, when hail damaged the head of the KOLS [infrared search and track system]. I directed the aircraft towards a brighter area behind the cloud from which we emerged into a sunny space. We engaged targets with unguided S-8 80mm rockets, targeting railway wagons and fuel tankers.

During that mission, our interlocutor's aircraft was hit by a round from small arms fire in the engine area, but without major consequences.

Due to the high value of the MiG-29s from the 127th Squadron, it was estimated that the loss of those planes should not be risked, and that is why the pilots of the 'brotherly' 126th Squadron flew combat missions with the MiG-2bis planes practically every day. Due to the limited tactical radius of the MiG-21bis they were usually striking targets up to the line connecting Donji Miholjac with Slavonski Brod. Even then, and except when operating against targets in Osijek, Vukovar, or Vinkovci, they still had to carry additional drop tanks on the outboard underwing stations. The most common combat loads included launchers for 57mm and 128mm rockets, S-24B 240mm rockets, BL755 cluster bombs, FAB-250 aerial bombs, and PLAB-350 napalm bombs. During nighttime missions, they first deployed two FAB-100MN flare bombs and then engaged with unguided rockets.

At least once, R-13M (ASCC/NATO codename 'AA-2D Advanced Atoll') infrared-homing, short-range air-to-air missiles were deployed to strike ground targets. Supplies of aerial bombs were limited due to high consumption, and there was a need to assess whether it made sense to use the R-13M as a homing missile. At that time, Croatian forces launched powerful attacks on barracks in Osijek, and the pilot took-off from Batajnica AB with a MiG-21bis carrying two missiles under its wings. Near the barracks, he found a suitable target for infrared-homing missiles – a metal roof reflecting strong sunlight – and launched both weapons. Although, according to the pilot's assessment, they hit the target, the use of R-13M was abandoned because it was too challenging to find suitable conditions for use, and the warhead was too weak for destroying ground targets.

In the fall of 1991, Galeb-4 aircraft from the 252nd Squadron were usually armed with four launchers for 57mm or 128mm rockets; alternatively with FAB-100, FAB-250, or Mk.82K slick bombs, Hunting BL755 cluster bombs or PLAB-200 napalm. A characteristic tactic involved the guiding of air attacks by forward air controllers, usually an experienced pilot of a higher officer rank. They observed positions, often from concealed locations in houses, and guided aircraft through radio communication. The third type of sortie flown were air strikes against targets recognised as valuable through aerial reconnaissance or reported as such by ground forces and intelligence gathering.

On some flights, thermobaric bombs designed at the Belgrade Military Technical Institute were used. Their original designation was ASB-250, an acronym in the Serbian language for a thermobaric bomb (aerosol bomb). To conceal the true purpose and myth that it was internationally banned ordnance, a later designation used was FAB-275 M91 with alphabetical prefixes for standard HE bombs (fragmentation aerial bomb). The platform for deploying these bombs was the Galeb-4 from the Air Test Centre, an institution directly subordinated to the deputy of the General Staff of the Armed Forces of the SFRJ for the RV i PVO, and responsible for final tests and evaluation of the quality of air force technology. Pilots and technicians from the Aviation Test Centre maintained a team at combat readiness, which carried out assigned missions according to orders from the I Corps RV i PVO.

One soldier, an ethnic Croat, attempted to sabotage a VOC Galeb-4 by shooting a rag that he dipped in jet fuel into the air inlet of the aircraft. He was caught and sentenced to four years in prison at a military court.

Jastrebs and Galebs were usually armed with old 5-inch rockets, best known as HVARs. Indeed, the ordnance deployed was almost exclusively unguided and the use of precision guided munitions like the AGM-65B Maverick and Grom was just a curiosity in statistical terms. A characteristic combat load on all models of combat aircraft were launchers for unguided rockets of the S-5 family – the Soviet-made S-5M with HE warhead and S-5K with HEAT (high-explosive anti-tank) warhead, or their equivalents BR-1-57 and BR-2-57 produced in the Krušik factory in Valjevo, in Serbia. The UB-32 launchers for 32 rockets and UB-16 launchers for 16 rockets were attached to the MiG-21's underwing pylons. For the Yugoslav Galeb-2s and Jastrebs, which had low ground clearance, launchers of reduced section for 12 L-57-12 were made.

A HVAR rocket under the wing of a Galeb-2 from the 252nd Squadron in flight over the Pannonian Plain. Eastern Slavonia and Baranja are flat areas covered with fields making it difficult for pilots to orientate at low altitudes. (Dragan Veličković)

A T-55A from the 453rd Mechanised Brigade in the area of Šid in summer 1991. (Zoran Sinko)

The focus of combat operations on the Slavonic battlefield was the city of Vukovar with its wider surroundings and the area oriented towards the city of Vinkovci. (Collection Ivan Detiček)

A MiG-29 armed for CAS mission with two B8M1 launchers for 20 80mm S-8KO rockets and two R-60MK infrared air-to-air missiles. (Aleksandar Radić collection)

Technicians from Tuzla air base prepping an Orao aircraft from the 241st Squadron for combat sorties on 1 November 1991. They are armed with L-57-016MD launchers for 16 unguided 57mm rockets. The left aircraft in the photograph, number 25154, was hit on 15 November with a Strela-2M missile, however the pilot made it back to the base. (Aleksandar Kelić)

In the RV i PVO during the war months, training of young pilots was still routinely conducted and is why part of every squadron was exempted from combat. From Tuzla air base, until 10 October, all Galeb-4s from two squadrons were redeployed to Golubovci air base. Instead of combat assignments pilots of these squadrons flew with students. At Tuzla, the war continued for the pilots of the Orao aircraft from the 241st Squadron. Based next to them were MiG-21PFMs from the 129th Squadron carrying out training of fighter pilots in their fourth year of schooling. Although this photograph was taken on 1 November, when Orao aircraft from the same base were flying on combat sorties, the cadets were flying on combat training with aircraft armed with UB-16-57 launchers for unguided 57mm rockets. Unlike the combat unit pilots who received new camouflage overalls in 1991 and had their pilot helmets repainted, the cadets and instructor flew in pre-war blue overalls and with white helmets. (Aleksandar Kelić)

Orao attack aircraft flew from Tuzla where there was no permanently stationed unit until the beginning of the war, however, there was the logistical 399th Air Base in charge of supporting any aviation unit that landed on their runway. (Aleksandar Kelić)

An Orao J-22 aircraft prepares for take-off for a combat mission On 1 November 1991. The wartime situation is confirmed by the pistol carried by the technician. (Aleksandar Kelić)

A detachment of Orao aircraft from the 241st Squadron on combat missions from 10 October to 8 December was primarily only armed with 57mm and 128mm unguided rockets. Only on a few occasions were Mk.82 500lb and FAB-250 bombs used. (Aleksandar Kelić)

The RV i PVO bases were not threatened by the Croatian armed forces, but combat security was on alert just in case. The Bofors L/70 40mm guns at the Tuzla base were an effective tool for anti-infantry combat. (MC Odbrana)

A pilot from the 252nd Squadron stands next to his Galeb-4 wearing the type of flight gear used for combat missions during 1991–1992. In addition to the prescribed camouflage jumpsuit, the pilot has added a vest from the M89 land force uniform. Visible on the pilot's PK-75 helmet, is the standard RV i PVO emblem with a red five-pointed star. (Aleksandar Radić)

The emblem of the 252nd Squadron "*Kurjaci sa Ušća*" was designed in the autumn of 1991. The insignia featured a winged wolf against a backdrop of blue sky, white surface, and the sun, using the colours of the Yugoslav tricolour. (Aleksandar Radić collection)

An HT-40E from the 678th Squadron, with the Aries-F system from the Italian company Elletronica, was used in the signals intelligence role. (Milorad Ristić)

The Osijek Region

Osijek – the biggest city in eastern Croatia – included a main military base known as the *Narodni heroj Milan Stanivuković* (referred to as the 'White Barracks'). This housed a reinforced battalion of the 12th Brigade. The Croatian 106th Territorial Defence Brigade, with reinforcements from the 3rd (regular) Brigade and the police, surrounded the barracks. They attempted their first attack on 14 September and were repelled. However, the next day, they demolished a wall on the west side of the barracks using TNT. The passage was not large enough but the Territorial Defence troops tried to break through, losing one fighter in the process, and the platoon commander was wounded. They were followed by a police intervention platoon, which entered and occupied one of the buildings. In response to the request of the 12th Brigade for air support, on 16 September, two MiG-21bis jets attacked with Munja rockets. Nevertheless, supported by a recoilless gun, the Croat police breached the barracks' fence and took control of its southeast part. The staff of the garrison assessed that the situation would soon be untenable, so they demolished part of the wall on the southwest side of the barracks and broke through Croatian positions with around 10 T-55A MBTs and two APCs, along with a few soft-skinned vehicles. The Croats destroyed two tanks, a Pinzgauer 4x4 light truck, and a medical vehicle.

Not everyone inside the barracks managed to break out and on 17 September, after a series of Croatian attacks, 226 members of the JNA surrendered. On the same day, parts of the 12th Brigade mounted on M-60PB APCs, broke through from Polygon C – a location at the southern edge of the city – towards the village of Tenja, held by the local Serbian militia.

In the battles for the Lug warehouse near Osijek, which was defended by an equivalent of two platoons, six M53/59 AA guns, and three M-60 APCs against an estimated force of 700 Croats, aircraft did not provide support despite multiple requests. In the early hours of 20 September 1991, 54 soldiers quietly left their trenches under the cover of fog and attempted to break through to the nearest JNA units. They were captured only two days later. For fear of airstrikes, the Croats quickly withdrew weapons from the warehouse, including six M48 76mm mountain guns and six M53/59 AA guns. The aircraft of the RV i PVO did finally appear to target the abandoned depot, but only on 21 September.[5]

The First Pilot POW

Croatian forces implemented the order for a complete blockade of barracks in all garrisons in the east of the country: Osijek, Našice, Vukovar, Vinkovci and Đakovo. Small units were easy prey: border posts from the 51st Border Battalion (XVII Corps) were located on the border between Yugoslavia and Hungary, which stretched along the Drava River. On the night of 15–16 September, the Croatian 107th Territorial Defence Brigade launched an attack on three border posts covering the Yugoslav-Hungarian border in the region of Donji Miholjac. Two posts surrendered, but fighting continued for the third where a battalion-sized task force from the 107th Brigade, reinforced by a single battery of 120mm mortars and a platoon of triple 20mm AA guns fought against the garrison of the barracks located in the town. At 0930hrs the barracks fell and around 70 officers, NCOs and soldiers were captured. There were no fatalities on either side in the skirmish, but one Croatian fighter was wounded. One of the soldiers allegedly complained, 'Where are the planes that were promised to us?'[6]

In the morning hours, two pilots from the 252nd Squadron were ordered to take-off on an armed reconnaissance mission and establish whose forces controlled the border posts. The leader of the pair, Captain Dragoslav Ranđelović, took-off in the J-21 numbered 24136, armed with four 5-inch HVAR rockets and two KPT-100 cluster bomb units (essentially, thin metal casings, each containing eight 16kg bomblets), plus 405 rounds for its three internally installed Browning 12.7mm/.50-cal AN/M3 machine guns. The two Jastreb fighters took-off from Batajnica at 09:30hrs, after the border post had already fallen. The pilots had difficulty with the morning fog and navigation while underway only 50 metres above the terrain. Eventually, they launched an attack on the border posts in Donji Miholjac. During the aiming phase, Randjelovic's aircraft, at an altitude of some several dozen metres, was hit by a round from an assault rifle, that pierced the cockpit. The pilot's lower leg was injured, but he returned for another attack. This was followed by a powerful explosion that almost cut the plane in half when it was hit by a missile from a Strela-2M MANPADS. One part of the aircraft fell on the shore of the lake near the town, and the tail fell into the water. Ranđelović ejected and landed near a pond at Orahovica. The second pilot of the pair, Captain Duško Vergas, manoeuvred to avoid a missile that was flying towards his plane, violating Hungarian airspace before continuing east and then back to the airport where he returned with only 40 litres of fuel.

The Croats launched a pursuit for Ranđelović, who recalled:

> I'm panting, I'm crawling, I'm running as far as I can. I fall into a deep ditch. Mud. Full boots… I scratch with my nails and drag myself to a willow bush, I creep in. Suddenly: peace… In the distance the barking of dogs and some unintelligible voices…I'm changing the magazine in the Scorpion,[7] I`m placing a bigger one. I have one bomb left, the other fell somewhere. The voices are getting closer. They are looking for me… They are already close, a few metres from me, but they don't see me. At that moment MiGs fly by, a pair. Bursts from all sides.[8] I hear a helicopter. It flies low, at less than ten metres. The bursts start again, they are shooting at it from all weapons. It flies right over me, but I can't raise for them to see me: they will shoot…. Peace again. They pass by, they don't detect me… I only heard the arrival of the second helicopter. If I had a flare, they might have seen me. With a leg full of shrapnel, scratched, muddy, I crawled and pulled up grass behind me to cover my tracks. I weaved my way between groups of pursuers until I found a bush thick enough to wait safely for night. Autumn cold rain, mosquitoes, thirst, hunger …
>
> I bandaged my leg. Terrible pain in my thigh – as I was crawling the flyers knife cut through the sheath and cut my skin in several places. I spent the night in constant motion. I crawled into the corn, slipped through canals, reeds, mud. Some remaining peppers and tomatoes in the already harvested gardens satiated my hunger a little. The dawn helped me to determine the east, to orient myself. I'm walking, I'm falling… The sky has clouded over, I'm losing my sense of the sides of the world. I'm going randomly … In the evening I come across water. I think River Drava. On the shore I find four to five boats, each tied with a chain. I take out the wooden floors from the bottom, tie them, and make a raft. At the crack of dawn I will cross the Drava. I spend the night in frenzy. A nightmare, the cold shakes me … Just before dawn I see that one boat has no chain. I tear off a board and crawl into it. I paddle feverishly, downstream, thinking it's the Drava. Suddenly, a reed. It's getting thicker and thicker. It's just a pond again … I turn back … I leave the boat, continue on foot. I

> come across water – a pond again. Ponds, ponds, constantly ponds. I wonder if I'm not in Hungary. Reed, mud, rain doesn't stop. I have no idea where I am, I'm walking at random. I was captured by the village guard in Podgorska Podgojca. I wanted to read, on a board by the road where I am. They spotted me .... They were fair to me, and then the members of the Ministry of the Interior arrived, armed to the teeth .... From there, the spitting, hitting, and questioning began.[9]

Ranđelović was captured after two days on the run. In front of him, the Croatian police officers discussed whether to kill the pilot on the spot or whether it was important to keep him safe. Luckily for Ranđelović, the side that believed he was more valuable alive prevailed and he was placed in Osijek prison. Randjelovic's colleagues from the 252nd Squadron launched an action to free him. Through private connections, they made contact with the Croatian side and negotiations were opened through telephone conversations routed via Osijek to Sobota, and when the telephone lines were cut off, by calls from Hungary. The Croats first asked for two of their own men for exchange, then raised the price to 10. The exchange was agreed and on 1 November 1991, Ranđelović crossed the bridge on the Vuka River between Ernestinovo and Petrova Slatina. The Croatian policeman who followed him said: 'You got life on the day of the dead…'

The action of exchanging Ranđelović for 10 Croats from the list that arrived from Osijek was protected by 252nd Squadron's planes that were in the air and a Gama helicopter from the 712th Squadron forward deployed in the village of Silvaš.[10]

Galeb-4 Down

The next day, 17 September 1991, another aircraft from the 252nd Squadron was shot down. Captain 1st Class Zoran Marjanović took-off in Galeb G-4 number 23603 from Batajnica for a mission in the Osijek area. He bombed the target with four Mk.82K aerial bombs with retarding devices for low-altitude release. In the Nemetin area, while crossing power lines at an altitude of about 100m, the aircraft was hit in the rear by a Strela-2M missile. The engine stopped. Marjanović continued to glide, descending gently while trying to fly towards the east to reach territories under the control of the local Serbian militia. Above Bijelo Brdo, he sharply turned the aircraft to the right to avoid falling into the village, and in horizontal flight at a speed of around 200km/h, rapidly descended towards the ground. He ejected from a height of about 50 metres. The plane crashed in Sarvaš.

Marjanović took cover in a cornfield and fired a shot from his M84 automatic pistol to check if it was working. He switched to burst mode, inserting a magazine of 20 rounds. Grenades began to fall around him. After about 10 minutes, he heard calls to respond. Not sure who the people in the cornfield were, he remained silent until they approached. They turned out to be members of the local Serbian militia. The pilot was transported by truck to their headquarters in the village of Vera, 15km from Bijelo Brdo, and after half an hour, a helicopter arrived under mortar fire and extracted him.

The area of Osijek proved to be very risky for aircraft as the Strela-2M missile operators were efficient, and they shot down a third aircraft on 17 October. Lieutenant Zoran Starčević, a pilot from the 252nd Squadron, took-off from Batajnica in J-21 Jastreb number 24116, armed with two launchers with BR-1 and BR-2 unguided rockets, four HVAR rockets and 405 rounds of 12.7mm ammunition. After losing two aircraft flying at low altitudes, the pilots switched to the so-called high-altitude attack scheme, reaching the target at an altitude of 4,000m. Starčević was a wingman in a pair of Jastreb aircraft tasked to operate in the Osijek–Tenja area, focusing on the Panonija transport company's area where numerous military vehicles had been observed.

The leader took action, and then Starčević pressed the firing button, but the munitions did not release from the pylon. He tried two more times to conduct the attack and began to pull out of the attack at an altitude of 1,200 metres and a speed of 700km/h. He turned in the direction of the village of Tenja, controlled by the Serbian militia, and climbed at a rate of 25m/s. Two seconds after he saw that he passed an altitude of 3,400 metres, Starčević felt a strong impact in the rear of the aircraft: his jet had been hit by a Strela-2M launched from Tufek, a suburb of Osijek that was part of the Croatian defence line. The aircraft turned upside down and departed controlled flight into a flat spin, on its back. The pilot released the control stick and saw that the engine thrust had dropped to 20 percent. He knew he had to eject immediately, but it was not easy to reach the ejection handle of the Folland Mk 1B ejection seat. At an altitude of about 1,000 metres, the pilot exited the aircraft, and the parachute opened. An eyewitness from the scene, Slavko Bugarski, said that the Croats were shooting at the pilot while he was on the parachute, and it was a miracle that he was not hit given the close range from which they were firing.

When he landed near the remains of the aircraft, he pulled out his M84 machine pistol and ran to the first field to take cover behind the vegetation. After about 10 minutes, he ran into combatants of the Tenja militia and went with them to the local HQ. Twenty minutes later, a Mi-8 from I Corps RV i PVO Aviation Department arrived for Starčević. The crew landed under Croatian mortar fire and extracted the downed pilot.

The Vukovar Tragedy

The fate of Vukovar in the Yugoslav Civil War reflected that era. A town stretching nearly 10 kilometres along the bank of the Danube River, with a centre renowned for its baroque architecture, had been almost completely obliterated by months-long shelling by the JNA and air strikes of the RV i PVO. During the pre-war census of 1991, Vukovar had population of 44,639, predominantly Croats, accounting for 47.18 percent, Serbs at 32.31 percent, and a distinct category labelled as Yugoslavs representing 9.75 percent. The Vukovar municipality had a total population of 84,189 people, 36,190 Croats and 31,445 Serbs. The Serbian militia was particularly strong in a place called Borovo, connected to Vukovar, which had around 6,500 residents, with 80 percent of them being Serbs.

The initial incidents between Croatian forces and Serbian militias in Borovo Selo, which is connected to Vukovar, gradually grew during the summer of 1991 into daily battles. Then, on 25 August, Croats successfully occupied the local barracks. The Croats firmly held the Vinkovci–Marinci–Nuštar axis to maintain contact with the forces in Vukovar. They attempted to surround all the barracks in the Sajmište district of the town, which provoked a strong reaction from the JNA. During the battles on 14–15 September, Croatian forces were repelled – amongst others by jets of the 126th and 252nd Squadrons. Federal forces gained control of the Vukovar–Vinkovci road, but they did not completely surround and isolate the battlefield. One crucial route remained in the hands of the Croats: Nuštar–Marinci–Bogdanovci–Vukovar. Four days later, the JNA also managed to recover the local military base.

Significant reinforcements for the Federal forces arrived in the last week of September when the Guards Motorised Brigade was deployed to the vicinity of Vukovar. This unit was rushed to the battlefield after an incident on 29 September 1991 in which a number of its officers NCOs, disgruntled by the developments on the battlefield, attempted to replace the Federal Secretary of the Army, General Kadijević. The following night, the unit was ordered to battle and directly subordinated to the Command of the 1st MD. From 2 October, street fighting involved members of the Guard, while parts of the 1st Proletarian Guards Mechanised Division arrived from Belgrade. Task Force South was formed on the basis of the Guards Motorised Brigade and became the main force in capturing Vukovar. In the north, Task Force North was formed from parts of the XII Corps. Both formations consisted of various units, mostly engaged on a battalion level.

Tail of Jastreb number 24136. (HMDCDR)

The initial JNA attempt to secure Vukovar failed. Therefore, from early October, it blockaded the town while sending forward detachments that gradually established control over the most important parts of the town south and north of the Vuka River. Next, the Federal forces began mopping up. The primary task of the air force was battlefield air interdiction in the context of maintaining the blockade, and close air support. Additionally, the Riverine Flotilla of the JNA was tasked with monitoring the Danube. Parts of the 1st Proletarian Guard Mechanised Division and the 252nd Armoured Brigade, which took the village of Marinci on 1 October, were responsible for cutting off the city from Vinkovci, blocking the route used for reinforcements and resources to Vukovar for a few days.

Inside Vukovar, the Croats organised defensive strongholds, with the main unit being the local brigade of the Territorial Defence – meanwhile redesignated as the ZNG. The ZNG unit officially responsible for Vukovar received the designation 124th Brigade, but its members referred to it as the 204th Brigade.

The Croats attempted to break the blockade of Nuštar–Marinci–Bogdanovci–Vukovar with simultaneous attacks from both sides. Reinforcements, including equipment captured from the JNA's XXXII Corps in Varaždin – seven T-55A MBTs, 11 M-80A IFVs, and six M36 self-propelled guns – arrived for this task. In turn, the RV i PVO ordered the aircraft from Batajnica AB to provide close air support. MiGs from the 126th Squadron carried out nine sorties on targets around and in Vinkovci, each equipped with two L-128-04MD launchers with four Munja rockets each, and one or two BL755 cluster bombs.

The Croatian attempt to break through on the night of 4–5 October, failed amid heavy artillery fire from the Federal forces. According to Croatian analyses, they misjudged the effective strength of the JNA, which included one armoured brigade and two others. Despite this, on the night of 5–6 October, they made another attempt and managed to secure control over the village of Nuštar. However, the crews of T-55A MBTs and M-80A IFVs refused to continue fighting, stating that 'the JNA, with intensive aviation and artillery action against Croatian forces, made it clear that it does not intend to leave the corridor so easily'.

In a new attack on 13 October, the Croats failed to overcome well-prepared positions of M-84 MBTs in the villages of Marinci, Cerić, and Henrikovac, and lost five T-55A MBTs.[11]

In mid-October, after the collapse of defence lines in the village of Lužac, on Sajmište Street and Trpinjska Cesta, the situation for Croatian forces in Vukovar became hopeless. From 24 October, the Croats used Antonov An-2 biplanes requisitioned to drop supplies into the besieged Vukovar. These had belonged to the company *Privredna Avijacija Osijek* before the war, but they were repainted in a camouflage scheme and had crews from the Croatian armed forces. The Croat An-2s flew by night while the RV i PVO ruled the skies by day, because it lacked navigational aids and ordnance suitable for precise air strikes in conditions of limited visibility.

One of the pilots from the 204th Regiment recalled a mission in which he dived his MiG-21bis from an altitude of about 4,000 metres, to release two FAB-250M-54 250kg bombs. One of them entered directly into a bunker near the Ovčara agricultural estate, 5km southeast of Vukovar, where Croatian soldiers were located. However, it did not detonate. From the Croatian side, a panicked voice was heard on the radio reporting that a bomb had smashed into the bunker.

Third Croat Attempt to Breakthrough

In addition to the Jastreb aircraft from the 252nd Squadron, shot down on 24 August in the battles around Vukovar, the RV i PVO also lost another jet. On 4 November 1991, Captain 1st Class Živojin Lazić took-off in aircraft serial number 24268 to attack positions of the ZNG southeast of the cathedral in Vukovar. He initiated the attack from an altitude of 2,800 metres, using four HVAR rockets and 32 unguided 57mm rockets. During the egress, he noticed a change in the sound of the engine, gradually losing thrust. The pilot attempted to shut down and restart the engine, but the thrust continued to decrease. While flying over Vojvodina in northern Serbia, in the area of Bačka Palanka, he jettisoned his rocket launchers. When assessing that he could not reach the airport through gliding, he ejected from an altitude of 200 metres at an instrument speed of 230km/h, two kilometres northeast of a farm at Kisač.

On 9 November 1991, the Croat forces attempted to break through to Vukovar for the third time. A combined force of the ZNG and police was tasked with assaulting the village of Karađičevo in the Vinkovci area. In the preparation for the action, the Croats estimated the presence of a platoon of 30 Serbian militiamen and a reinforced platoon of 30–40 JNA troops, including two tanks – a T-55 and a T-34/85. They planned to undertake the attack through 'concentric actions of sabotage-ambush groups from multiple sides simultaneously'. The main task was assigned to a special police squad from Varaždin, which, at the very beginning of the battle at 0600hrs, ran into a minefield and came under intense machine gun fire.

At that point in time, M-84 tanks of the JNA appeared in the village, prompting the Croats to send forward their own tank unit, while infantry – which was under constant artillery shelling – began to construct a fortified line stretching from Durgutovica via Borinci to Jarmina.[12]

Tasked with locating and engaging a reported Croat tank column on the Mrzović–Jarmina road, aircraft took-off from Batajnica. The leader of the Galeb-4 pair from the 252nd Squadron was Major Novak Novaković, flying the aircraft 23734 armed with four launchers for 128mm unguided rockets. During the flight to Vukovar, the pair ascended to 4,500 metres and passed south of the target zone before turning around to attack from the south. After passing Vinkovci heading north-west, they reached Jarmina and initiated a search for targets. They discovered a tank column and began a descent at an angle of about 40 degrees. Fifteen Munja rockets were launched by Novaković (one rocket failed to launch). He pulled up the aircraft energetically, and at an altitude of about 2,800 metres, he turned around in the cockpit to survey the effects of his run – when he noticed the activity of anti-aircraft artillery hidden in the forest at Durgutovica.[13] During the ascent, he did not feel an impact, but upon checking his instruments, he observed that the engine thrust had dropped to about 50 percent. He increased the flight altitude to 3,500 metres. There was a strong smell of kerosene in the cabin and the engine was vibrating heavily, and the sound changed. The fuel gauge dropped to the minimum. Novaković continued to fly to the east, towards the Danube in order to eject over friendly territory. The engine stopped working due to lack of fuel when he was above the Bačka Palanka area, and the pilot ejected safely at an altitude of around 400 metres.

The Fall of Vukovar

The end of the Battle of Vukovar began on 10 November 1991 when the JNA and Serbian militias captured Bogdanovci, severing the last communication line to the besieged garrison. The final attempts of the Croatian counteroffensive and lifting the blockade of Vukovar collapsed in the face of tanks, during the following days. Late on 12 November, Croatian forces initiated an attack along the Cerić–Henrikovac–Marinci line, and in depth towards Bogdanovci. This effort was poorly coordinated however, and some of units did not even reach their starting positions, while forces deployed in Nuštar were counterattacked from two sides and from the air and forced to withdraw towards the village of Marinci. On 15 November, the Croat 131st Brigade of the ZNG came under attack of the 3rd Mechanised Brigade of the JNA and air strikes of the RV i PVO, and was forced to withdraw from several villages. Indeed, the Federal and Serbian forces continued their advance and on 16 November captured the village of Nijemci.

During the following night, the command of the Vukovar garrison clandestinely evacuated the ruined town. Additional troops managed to break out on the night from 17 to 18 November, but the remaining troops in the town began surrendering. By the time the JNA secured Borovo on 19 November, the last Croat combatants in Vukovar had given up.[14]

By then, following 48 days of intensive fighting, massive volumes of shelling by artillery, and air strikes, Vukovar was completely devastated. For the Serbs and Federals, it was a pyrrhic victory: the Croats demonstrated great determination and flexibility in urban combat, while the other side experienced widespread confusion, frequent interference at various levels in the command chain, and

The battles for Vukovar were compared to Stalingrad by the world media, but in a Balkan manner. From the last days of August to mid-November 1991, Federal forces and the TO of Krajina engaged in heavy fighting against Croatian forces, often house-to-house. A soldier observing the area from a destroyed house is wearing a camouflage cover, with printed desert and green-coloured spots, over his uniform. He is armed with an M70B1 assault rifle. (Vilijam Horvat)

The gloomy atmosphere of the destroyed city of Vukovar after the battle ended in November 1991. The characteristic water tower is the symbol of the city. (Vilijam Horvat)

mass desertions: not just battalions, but entire brigades had left their positions. Ironically, the image of the destroyed city was widely attributed to 'air power', i.e. the RV i PVO. Indeed, the War Chief of Staff of the Command of RV i PVO, Lieutenant General Živan Mirčetić, explained in an interview years after the war: '... given the time available – considering that winter was approaching – the city could not be taken without significant and intense air force action. My opinion is that it was excessive, and the city suffered a catastrophe largely due to the excessive use of the air force.' Commander of the 1st MD, Lieutenant General Života Panić, in a post-war response to a journalist's question about why the battles for the city continued after the blockade of the military units had been lifted, said that the blockade had been lifted, but there was constant enemy action directed at the barracks, 'Even if we lifted the blockade of the barracks, it didn't mean we were completely at peace. Attacks on the barracks and JNA members were constant, and that's why we had to complete that task.'[15]

Every day, the wounded from the battle for Vukovar were transported from Negoslavci to the VMA by Mi-8. Crews, like the flight technician NCO in the photo, were exposed to the risk of being hit by infantry weapons and therefore wore ballistic vests and helmets. (Vilijam Horvat)

An NCO from the RV i PVO's 'combat camera' team poses with a Soviet-made M39 37mm anti-aircraft gun. It was obsolete in its originally intended role but was of great use to the TO in street fighting. (Vilijam Horvat)

The remains of Jastreb number 24268, shot down on 4 November 1991, burning in a field near the Kisač agricultural facility. (RV i PVO)

Some Gazelles were offered to the ECMM and had white surfaces on the tail boom. The observers also had Dutch Alouette IIIs, but the Yugoslav Gazelles continued to fly with white surfaces. One of them, H-45 number 12894 from the 890th Squadron, arrived for liaison duties on 16 October 1991, in the village of Negoslavci, where the command of the forces fighting for Vukovar was located. (Tanjug)

Isolation of the Battlefield

In early November, the command of the Croatian armed forces for Eastern Slavonia assessed that Vukovar was on the verge of falling and that once the JNA occupied the city, it could continue further and cut off Osijek. Under the pressure of a potential front collapse, President Tuđman directly requested the reinforcement of the defence in the eastern Croatia by additional brigades. On 10 November 1991, the main headquarters of the Croatian army decided to send the 105th Brigade of the ZNG from Bjelovar, because this was the only fully-equipped unit not engaged in combat at that point in time. Overenthusiastic, the HQ of Eastern Slavonija conceived that the additional brigade could seize the village of Bogdanovci, break through the encirclement around Vukovar, defeat the JNA and Serbian militias, and thus lift the blockade of the town.[16]

Some units of the 105th Brigade at the time of the concentration of forces were in the villages around Đakovo. The brigade was ordered to reach the starting positions by 12 November, and moved in a marching column to the east, even though Bogdanovci had been under the control of the Federals and Serbs since 10 November.[17]

Reconnaissance flights by the RV i PVO identified heavy military traffic along the road from Našice to Đakovo. In pursuit of the Croatian vehicles in transit, at 1435hrs on 12 November, a pair of MiG-21bis from the 126th Squadron took-off from Batajnica AB. The leader was Lieutenant Colonel Miroslav Vidaković, chief of staff and deputy commander of the 204th Regiment, a highly experienced pilot with significant combat experience. Under the wings of his aircraft, serial number 17156, were four launchers with 96 57mm unguided rockets loaded into two UB-32-57s with 32 rockets each, and two UB-16-57s with 16 rockets each. He also had a full ammunition load of 250 rounds for the internally installed GSh-23 gun of his jet. On the central pylon was a fuel tank with a capacity of 490 litres. His wingman in the other MiG-21bis had two launchers with four 128mm rockets each.

Vidaković recalled flying at an altitude of 4,000 metres, and when they noticed the column near Nabrđe, they initiated a dive:

> We started late, so we pushed the angle, I fired rockets at the column, pulled the aircraft up, but not quickly enough because the large pods for 32 rockets prevented us from going faster than 750km/h. When the 'belovke' cluster bombs (slang for British-made Hunting BL755) were released, as soon as they detached, the speed could be increased to 900–1,000km/h. Then I was hit; the engine stopped, and the plane quickly descended. The speed was dropping, and I ejected at a low altitude. I had no more than 500km/h at that moment. I heard the blast of the parachute opening. The ground was approaching, but they were shooting at me from below, 10–15 soldiers.

Fortunate not to be hit, Vidaković landed near the village of Novi Perkovci, outside Đakovo, and decided to attempt a breakout to the Sava River, over which he could escape into Bosnia and Herzegovina. The headquarters of his unit was informed about his ejection a minute after it took place: at 1505hrs. His wingman did not see what happened but heard Vidaković's corresponding message over the radio. Because Vidaković landed too far from the positions of the JNA and Serbian militias, there was no chance of organising a search and rescue operation. Thus, Vidaković was on his own while trying to escape towards the Sava. First, he reached the Zagreb–Belgrade railway line, where he needed to cross two tracks: he knew that the river was nearby. Encountering a patrol, he heard the question, 'Who goes there?' and responded bluntly, 'a peasant.' They opened fire, and Vidaković dived into a cornfield. He watched three soldiers near the railway who occasionally fired randomly. Waiting patiently until the Croat patrol distanced, he then observed the passage of three trains before seizing the opportunity to continue further. His goal was Slavonski Šamac and then to somehow cross the bridge over the Sava and reach Bosanski Šamac. At dusk, he flagged down a truck with Macedonian license plates. He openly addressed the driver, revealed who he was, and requested a ride across the river. The driver invited Vidaković to enter the cabin and casually assured him not to worry; they would cross the bridge. Ahead of them was a column of trucks waiting for inspection, and the driver went to see what was happening. Vidaković, dressed in a camouflage flight suit, attempted to conceal himself as much as realistically possible.

About 10 minutes later, three members of the ZNG ran towards the truck, making it clear that the Macedonian driver had reported his passenger. Vidaković quickly exited the cabin, leaving behind an M84 automatic pistol, and ran towards the village amidst the sounds of an alarm siren: 'I ran through the darkness and bumped into three or four of them, and they caught me and took me to the bridge to the container checkpoint. They took-off my flight suit and leather jacket and gave me a SMB uniform.'

Late on 15 November, he was transported to Slavonski Brod with a couple of bumps: 'In the morning, an aggressive captor appeared, grabbed me by the hair, and put a bayonet to my throat, talking about how he had slaughtered three during the Second World War, and now I was to become the fourth.' The intimidation continued, but in the meantime, a van from Osijek arrived, into which he was bundled, tied up. They drove him to Đakovo, where the escorts rested at the police station, while Vidaković was struck in the back with an automatic rifle: 'From the impact, I flew into the cell. Later, someone threw a hand grenade; it hissed and didn't explode.'

Vidaković ended his first day in captivity in Osijek, where the torture began. His Croat captors beat him with electrical cables and boots; he passed out, and then they poured water on him to wake him up and continued to torment him. After the first treatment, they dragged him into a cell with multiple injuries – they had broken his collarbone, three ribs, and he had injuries all over his legs. The cell was nothing but concrete and a plank for sleeping. They came for him routinely and continued with the beatings. One of the torturers put a revolver in Vidaković's mouth and said he would kill him. One of them held a grudge because his sister had died in an air strike, although it later turned out that the story was not entirely correct: the sister died when a Strela-2M missile fired at several aircraft of the RV i PVO failed, and crashed into a home, killing the woman in question. On 1 December, Vidaković was handed over to the JNA at Pleso AB as part of a POW exchange. He remembers how he requested a cigarette from a soldier at the base entrance, then had two or three glasses of whiskey at the airport headquarters and boarded an An-26 that transported him to Batajnica AB.

Subsequent investigation revealed that Vidaković's aircraft was targeted by a Strela-1M (ASCC/NATO codename 'SA-9 Gaskin') that was protecting the march of the 105th Brigade towards Vukovar. Gunner Dražen Slavnić recalled being in a field near Đakovo when an observer from the crew's vehicle reported an approaching aircraft. In the first attack, the MiG targeted the location of the 105th Brigade but missed. It circled for a new attack, reduced its altitude, and entered the range of the missiles. Slavinić said:

> I heard the pulsating on the headphones, which was a sign that the plane was coming into range. When that sound stretched into a monotonous tone, something like when a person dies, and you only hear the whistling from the monitor, that's how I heard it, and I launched the missile. Based on the sound I received, I think it was at an altitude of about 3 to 3.5 kilometres.[18]

Friendly Fire

One incident involving friendly fire became the reason for a shift in one of the highest positions in the JNA – that of the Commander, 1st MD. In mid-September 1991, newly mobilised forces, including two powerful joint tactical units – the 2nd Proletarian Guard Mechanised Division and the 252nd Armoured Brigade equipped with M-84 and T-55A MBTs and M-80 IFVs – were concentrating in the town of Šid in western Srem, Serbia. They crossed the border to Croatia that was, at that time, an insignificant administrative line within the SFRJ, and were given the task of capturing the village of Tovarnik. On 20 September, two MiG-21bis aircraft targeted a transmitter in that village each using eight Munja 128mm rockets. The next day, one aircraft conducted a visual reconnaissance mission along the route Tovarnik–Vinkovci–Vukovar near Opatovac, the former base of Croatian forces that had been razed by aviation during the summer. The pilot spotted a column of military and civilian vehicles. The Command of the 1st MD received a report about the discovered column, and informed the HQ of the RV i PVO that there were no JNA forces in that area and action should be taken. Multiple times, the 1st MD requested verification from the Chief of Staff, Lieutenant General Andrija Silić, but they were assured, 'they are Ustašas, hit them'.[19]

The unit turned out to be the 208th Mixed Artillery Regiment – a reserve unit from Valjevo, in Serbia. It was targeted by two MiG-21s and the attack killed five soldiers and wounded dozens with their bombs. An injured officer, traumatised by the experience, subsequently committed suicide in hospital. What is more, demoralised by this air strike, reservists from the 2nd Proletarian Mechanised Division deserted en masse: more than 2,800 returned home to Valjevo and its surroundings, the brigade's peacetime location and where its mobilisation bases were situated. They left their combat equipment in the region of Šid. Later, the brigade was replenished, consolidated, and returned to the front. This event led to the removal of the commander of the 1st MD, who was of Macedonian ethnicity, and his deputy, an ethnic Croat. At that time, the ethnicity of the new commanders became important for the overall atmosphere in what remained of the JNA.

Fall of Orao

An important garrison in the central part of Slavonia was located in Đakovo, a place with about 20,000 inhabitants, over 90 percent of whom were Croats. The local barracks housed the equipment of the 158th Mixed Anti-Armour Artillery Brigade of the JNA: a unit armed for a defensive war with anti-tank guns and missile launchers, howitzers and air defence systems. The main barracks was situated in the Dračice District; the so-called 'small barracks' (a warehouse) was in the Gaj forest, while nearby there was the Nabrđe training ground. In the first attempt to seize these three locations, launched on 15 September, the Croats failed amid a fierce but chaotic effort. On the next day, they refocussed on the 'small barracks', defended by the equivalent of a platoon: this was eventually captured, but meanwhile the artillery from the Dračice barracks targeted Croatian positions in the city centre.

On 17 September, the Croats occupied the warehouse in Gaj and quickly organised the transport of weapons and ammunition by trucks to several locations because they expected retaliation from the RV i PVO. They were informed by the security service officer of the JNA, Lieutenant Colonel Sefer Halilović[20] that they must clear the warehouse within two days, because then aviation would rocket Đakovo. To their good fortune, on 18 September, the JNA garrison surrendered. Nevertheless, around 1803hrs local time, the air force –

ordered to destroy any heavy equipment left behind – conducted an air strike. The task was assigned to pilots from the 242nd Squadron, equipped with J-22 Orao fighter-bombers. The leader of the first pair that launched from Tuzla AB was Lieutenant Colonel Muše Begić, commander of the 172nd Regiment. At the time when the war started, he was one of the most experienced pilots of attack aviation with over 3,600 flight hours recorded in his flight book, including about 200 hours on the Orao.

Begić led in a two-seater NJ-22 Orao number 25508. His companion followed him in a staggered formation over Đakovo. In the first attack, they surprised the Croats and the commander opened fire from his two L-57-16 launchers for 57mm unguided rockets and two L-128-4s with eight 128mm Munja rockets. Begić immediately pulled into a climb, but seconds later was hit by a single Strela-2M. Both engines seized and there was no choice but to eject. After reaching an altitude of 400m, the pilot ejected at around 1820hrs, about 6,000 metres outside Đakovo (the exact place of the plane crash was north-east, near the village of Forkuševci):

> As soon as the parachute filled with air, I came to my senses and realised that I was being shot at in bursts. My stomach was sick with fear … I landed on the ground, I'm not bleeding, but it's hard to move. Spine! I'm crawling, with difficulty, leaving the parachute in the field and I'm hiding in a dried canal. I know: soon Kalashnikov barrels will be pointed at my forehead. I'm thinking: the pistol is here, I close my eyes and…? Before my eyes – a picture of my family. It's worth living, fighting. Hope is always the last to die. Zengas are arriving, they are cursing the Chetnik mother, the Serbian mother.[21] The pilot is lying low, a few steps away from them. And – powerless. It hurts. The commands are coming: Surrender, drop your weapons! I am wounded, I will not shoot! – I replied and peeked out from the sedge. Some of them immediately jumped to strangle me, but backed down before their leader's command that I must stay alive, because that was the order.

The Croats captured Begić and in a euphoric atmosphere during the first days of the open war against the JNA, TV cameras recorded his response to the question 'Would you send an appeal to your colleagues not to shoot and bomb Croatia?' Begić, even though he was in the hands of the enemy, replied: 'No, because they are carrying out their tasks, just like you, here. I would call on all the powerful people to stop this war'. A question followed; 'Do you know that it is a war crime, and that many officers will be war criminals, and that they will be tried, someday?'. Begić answered briefly 'I know!' To the question: 'When you heal a little bit, or – if they let you go, would you fly again on the same mission?!' Begić agreed with a resolute 'YES'. Begić was taken to Đakovo and then to Osijek, first for an examination at the hospital, where an injury to the second lumbar vertebra and a fracture of three ribs on the right side were found. He was taken to the police station and later testified that he was exposed to beatings, swearing and threats there. Begić was in captivity for 67 days. He was then transferred from Osijek to Zagreb and joined a larger group that was handed over to the JNA on 25 November 1991. They were transported aboard an Antonov An-26 from Pleso to Batajnica airport.

That said, the seizure of the JNA garrison of Đakovo was a giant victory for the Croats. Certainly enough, they suffered the loss of four killed and 26 wounded, while killing two from the JNA and wounding 16. However, a total of 84 Federal officers and 298 other ranks were captured. Within the local military base and at the Nabrđe training grounds, the Croats found large quantities of equipment, including 36 100mm T-12 anti-tank guns, 18 122mm M38 howitzers, 14 M42 (ZIS-3) guns, four M48 76mm mountain howitzers, 18 BOV-1 anti-tank armoured vehicles, and 18 BOV-3 anti-aircraft self-propelled guns, in addition to vast quantities of ammunition and 5,000 personal firearms.[22]

The burning remains of NJ-22 Orao number 25508, filmed by a cameraman recording the consequences of a Strela-2M missile hit. (Boris Gregurić collection)

Slavonski Brod

The JNA garrison of Slavonski Brod consisted of the 670th Pontoon Battalion, which surrendered to the local 108th Brigade of the ZNG. About 20km north of the town there was a connection node at the top of Degman Hill (461 metres above sea level), at the peak of Dilj Gora. In the first wave of the JNA blockade, the Croatian armed forces tried to occupy this position with a single platoon of infantry and two M-84A MBTs, but the defence – equivalent to one platoon – held its ground.[23] The JNA then rushed members of the Sabotage Detachment to the scene: they were delivered by a single Mi-8 helicopter, supported by air strikes from J-21s, and significantly strengthened the isolated position.

For a while after, the sole connection to the completely surrounded miniature garrison of Dilj Gora was maintained by air. Then the situation was assessed as too dangerous and the decision was taken to evacuate this exposed position. On 4 October 1991, the crews of three Mi-8 helicopters from the 890th Squadron took-off from Batajnica on a flight to Degman. One of the pilots participating in this mission, Mitar Ilkić, recalled that everyone was aware of the challenges they faced, and no one volunteered to take-off. Therefore, mixed crews were selected from the 890th Squadron and the 787th Squadron from Niš, which had a detachment with four pilots and two flight technicians attached to the Batajnica-based squadron. In case they needed to defend themselves against ground attack, the Mi-8 helicopters were armed with four UB-16-57 launchers for 57mm unguided rockets. The crews were equipped with body armour in addition to the standard Zastava M84 7.65mm automatic pistols; they also received M70 automatic rifles with six magazines and two hand grenades. In the lead Mi-8, number 12245, the first pilot was Captain Zoran Andrejić from the 890th Squadron, and the second pilot was Captain Zoran Latković from the 787th Squadron. Participating from the Batajnica squadron was flight technician Sergeant Milorad Krasić.

The take-off was delayed twice, and finally, the three 'eights' were in the air at around noon. Initially, they flew the route Batajnica–Sremska Mitrovica–Modriča–Brčko over 'friendly' territory, recalled Ilkić, who was in the cabin of an Mi-8 with his colleague Bogdan Dekić. After flying over Brčko, they cocked their weapons and then crossed the Sava River at an altitude of 30 metres, near the village of Donji Svilaj. From there, the formation continued straight in the direction of Dilj. Following an uneventful flight, the three helicopters landed at the position and embarked the entire garrison and its most important pieces of equipment. Once everybody was on board, the helicopters took-off again.

The original plan was to return via Slavonski Brod because the pilots estimated that this would surprise the Croatian air defences. However, Andrejić changed his mind and ordered everybody to follow exactly the same route along which they had reached Dilj, with a separation of about five seconds between individual helicopters. Once airborne, the three Mi-8s spaced as ordered and then flew at an altitude of 30 metres towards the Sava River east of Slavonski Brod. Ilkić recalled that near the village of Donji Andrijevci, the flight leader jinked his helicopter upwards, in order to fly above a high-tension wire, and then – to his right – saw a vehicle and 'equipment' he had not seen on the way in. Moments later, he and his crewmen heard shots and felt the impact of multiple rounds. Then somebody called on the radio, 'Number 1, your right engine is afire!' Looking to the front of him, Ilkić saw a red and orange flame coming out of the right engine of the lead Mi-8. Then the helicopter entered a climb, before suddenly diving behind a slope and disappearing behind treetops: the helicopter crashed between the villages of Oprisavci and Poljanic. To the right of shocked Ilkić, his co-pilot Dekić pulled their Mi-8 into a climb, and then started turning right to attack with his unguided rockets. Ilkić disagreed: 'At that moment, I took the controls, corrected our route and turned south flying at such a low level, we hit the tops of several trees with windows at the bottom front of our cabin'.

Dekić accepted the decision of his colleague and let him steer the Mi-8 in the direction of the Sava River, as Ilkić recalled: 'I saw the river in front of us and we continued in that direction at extremely low altitude over the ground. Various systems and signals blinked on the instrument panel and indicated multiple failures on the damaged machine'.

All the while concerned they might get 'hit by a Stinger' – referring to the US-made FIM-92 Stinger MANPADs known to have been acquired by the Croats – Ilkić eventually nursed his badly damaged Mi-8 across the river on one engine. Eventually, he was forced to make a landing in a field outside Donji Svilaj. Upon exiting

Mi-8 number 12247 from Batajnica`s 890th Squadron was used for medical evacuation tasks in Eastern Slavonia. In 1991, it was not unusual for an Mi-8 to have a Red Cross marking and UB-16 launchers for 57mm rockets. On combat missions, those rockets were used only on a couple of occasions in the crisis in Slovenia. (Milorad D. Ristić)

the machine, the crew and passengers counted a total of 16 hits. The third helicopter landed next to them, to check upon everybody's wellbeing, before continuing for Batajnica. About an hour later, a Gazelle arrived to pick up the crew of the badly damaged Mi-8 and transfer it back to base. Nothing similar was possible for the crew of Andrejić's helicopter, number 12245: its three members, as well as four NCOs that were on board as passengers evacuated from Dilj, were all killed. According to official Croatian sources, the three Mi-8s were hit by fire from personal weapons of the 3rd Company, I Battalion, 108th Brigade of the ZNG.[24] Unofficial Croat sources stress that the helicopters stumbled into a unit that had stopped in that area because its troops had heard the engine noise. The rest of the Degman garrison managed to evacuate its positions on 19 October 1991: they destroyed all the equipment they could not take with them, then made their way to the Sava River and crossed it in several boats.

The remains of the destroyed Mi-8 number 12245, recognisable just by the burnt gearbox. (Nenad Šetina)

Under war conditions, those killed in action were buried with military honours with the Yugoslav flag over their coffin. Pilot Zoran Andrejić, who lost his life in the downed Mi-8, was buried according to the procedure usual in the JNA with a Puch G cross-country vehicle and a coffin carried on a gun carriage. (Vilijem Horvat)

Liaison Gazelles

Gazelle pilots from 1/896th Squadron flew mainly on liaison and reconnaissance tasks supporting command and control of the land forces. The first and only task of transporting the wounded was during the initial battles, when pilot Zoran Novković transported a reserve officer from Erdut to the Military Medical Academy (*Vojnomedicinska akademija*, VMA) aboard a Gazelle. He later carried out a large number of liaison flights on behalf of the Command of the 1st MD:

> We had one Gazelle helicopter in Karađorđevo (near the village was an internal military hunting ground for high-ranking officials and foreign guests). From there, they flew for the needs of the forward command post of the 1st MD in the nearby village of Mladenovo to the command post in the village of Negoslavci south of Vukovar and units in the field deployed in the villages. Then, there were frequent flights from the district command in Belgrade to the front line.

One pilot and one technician pilot were usually rotated every seven days. Due to the risk of being shot down, the aircraft were usually flown along roads that were easy to recognise and navigate. From the town of Šid, flights were conducted along the road towards Vinkovci, which was under Croatian control, but at the fork in the road to Vukovar, they turned right and halfway from the intersection was the most frequent destination of the flights; the village of Negoslavci. The road was followed at extremely low altitudes, usually just two or three metres. When it was necessary to fly over open terrain, power lines were jumped over and then the nose of the Gazelle dropped down quickly to get out of sight of the enemy. Due to the lack of information about where the front lines were, it was crucial to monitor them and constantly follow the developments. That is why the crews immediately after returning from their task informed their colleagues what they saw on the roadside, especially where the artillery batteries were and in which direction the howitzers were pointed. It was estimated that there was a risk of running into artillery fire. On one flight, from the village of Dalj along the River Danube and towards the south, Novković had to transport Lieutenant General Života Panić, commander of the 1st MD, another general and a journalist to whom they wanted to show the activities of the JNA:

> Panić asked us to come closer to Vukovar where fierce fighting was going on. I flew at 2–3 metres and followed the situation on the left bank of the Danube towards Vojvodina, from where my colleagues with the Gama were operating. I was interrupted by the image of a Maluytka anti-tank missile tracer flying across the river towards the Croatian position in front of the nose of my Gazelle. I saw the Gama pulling out of the attack, but I didn't know if it was the first, second or fourth in the group that was in action. Ignoring the general's request, I directed my Gazelle towards the Vojvodina side of the Danube.

The HN-45M (SA.342L) Gamas from the 712th Anti-Tank Squadron were deployed in the Vukovar area. From Niš, four Gazelles (Gama and utility version) were deployed to Batajnica from 26 August to 22 November. In the statistics of the unit, 32 combat missions with 30 fire actions were recorded, with a total of 89 missiles used. Gazelles from 4/890th Squadron and the Liaison Aviation Squadron flew on liaison tasks in Eastern Slavonia for the RV i PVO. Their flights were often on identical routes as the 896th Squadron, but for the transport of air force officers.

Pilot Zoran Novković is seen here on the left next to his Gazelle, serial number 12672. On the right, in camouflage overalls, is his technician Petar Komadina. The officer in the middle is in the military blue uniform of the RV i PVO, which seemed anachronistic in the conflict in the fall of 1991. (Vilijam Horvat)

One of the frequent users of Gazelle flights in Slavonia and Srem was Lieutenant General Života Panić, commander of 1st MD, recognisable by his stocky build. He is welcomed by the infamous Major Veselin Šljivančanin, security service officer of the Guards Motorised Brigade. (RV i PVO)

Both of the RV i PVO's Aloutette IIIs were photographed here in the first half of 1991 in the smart scheme which they kept during the war months. They were used for routine liaison duties. (Dragan Veličković)

Police Helicopters in the War

Pilots from the Secretariat for Internal Affairs of Serbia took part in medevac operations. The unit that was based in Belgrade had a detachment in Novi Sad in which our interlocutor Sorin Lapadat was flying at that time. When the security situation became complex in May 1991, he was flying Bell 206L-1 Long Ranger II registration number YU-HBS and Bell 206B Jet Ranger III YU-HBU on reconnaissance missions along the border with Croatia. In the period of 20 May to 10 July he had 18 such sorties. The development of the crisis and increasingly fierce fighting shifted the tasks to the transport of the wounded. He flew Bell 206Bs with registrations YU-HBW and YU-HBX. He took-off from Novi Sad with a stretcher that was placed inside the aircraft to the village on the left bank of the Danube where the wounded from the front line were loaded. In the field, landing sites were chosen on the northern part of the front near Bogojev, the central part near the towns of Vajska and Živa, and in the south near Šid.

The wounded were transported to Novi Sad or to the VMA in Belgrade for medical care. On the first missions, a nurse was brought on board next to the pilot, but it turned out that they did not handle the flight well. That is why a technician from the air unit was trained to hold a bottle with an infusion and to take care of the wounded that were prepared for transport by the medics on the ground. These were routine tasks and from 1 August to 18 September, Sorin had 50 medical evacuation flights or terrain reconnaissance and fly-overs related to those tasks entered in his flight log.

Crash of a Gazelle Helicopter With a General

One Gazelle helicopter, number 12881, was lost on 13 November on a reconnaissance flight. The deputy commander of the 896th Squadron took-off from the forward command post of the 1st MD with the commander of the area, Lieutenant General Života Panić. The plan was to carry out a visual reconnaissance along the route Mladenovo–Rajićev Salaš–Borovo selo–Bršadin–Borovo selo–Tovariševo–Mladenovo, mostly in the area of combat operations, at an altitude of 10 to 20 metres above the ground at a speed of 200km/h. General Panić decided to return when they were in the traverse of Vukovar near the level bank of the Danube because he estimated that he had seen enough to assess the situation. When they were returning, the pilot noticed some technical problems and made an emergency landing three kilometres north of Mladenovo. On landing, the Gazelle rolled onto its right side. Both occupants came away without major injuries. It was estimated that the most likely cause of the accident was pilot error; insufficient attention during landing. The possibility of the passenger moving the flight controls involuntarily, and that the pilot did not notice it and was therefore surprised by the aircraft's behaviour was not entirely excluded.

H-45 number 12881 was damaged beyond the cost of repairs in the landing accident. (RV i PVO)

BARCS INCIDENT

During the night of 27 October, between 2048 and 2055hrs, one MiG-21bis aircraft dropped two BL755 cluster bombs on the Hungarian town of Barcs, located on the Drava River, whose course marks the inter-state border. The impact points of the HEAT submunitions covered an area of 386m in length and a maximum width of 96m, which approximately corresponds to the declared characteristics of the BL755, covering an area of 300x150m. Fifteen unexploded bomblets were found. According to Hungarian analyses of the events, air surveillance, utilising six radar positions (the main sensor being the P-37 air surveillance radar and PRV-13 height-finder radar from the Homokszentgyörgy site), tracked the aircraft formation from 2044hrs, with the direction and target being Virovitica. At 2047hrs, a trace of the aircraft leaving the formation was noticed, flying at an altitude of 3,500m at 600km/h towards the Hungarian border and was tracked until 2052hrs. The aircraft performed a manoeuvre changing direction and altitude, disappeared from the radar screen for one minute, and was again tracked from 2053hrs on a southbound course. According to Hungarian analyses, the pilot executed a combat turn and, according to eyewitnesses, dropped cluster bombs from approximately 300m, causing material damage to the local cemetery and houses. When the aircraft headed south, Hungarian border guards reported hearing the sound of AA guns. According to air surveillance estimates, it entered approximately 2.2km into Hungary.

From the Yugoslav side, it was confirmed that from 2025 to 2044hrs aircraft operated in the vicinity of Virovitica at an air distance of 10km from the Hungarian border with flare bombs and then HE and cluster bombs and rockets. It is stated that the aircraft armed with BL755s completed the attack at 2044hrs above Virovitica and that it was under constant radar control and that it did not enter the airspace of the neighbouring country. According to official Hungarian data on 27 October, two more violations of Hungarian airspace were detected and both times Hungarian MiG-21s were scrambled, but did not reach the target in time.

Hungarian authorities strongly protested the attack with cluster bombs. The first reaction was stormy; on 30 October, the then Prime Minister József Antall travelled to Barcz with two Mi-8s that followed two Mi-24s and a large delegation including all eight members of the parliamentary board for defence, Chief of General Staff, and deputy for the Air Force and Air Defence Major General Béla Balogh, journalists and military attachés. After the political show, a joint team for analysis was formed, composed of representatives of both air forces and representatives of the ministries of foreign affairs. On 12 November the commander of RV i PVO Lieutenant General Jurjević hosted the commander of the Hungarian Air Force, Major General János Urbán, at a meeting in Subotica.

The problem was resolved in a gentlemanly manner acceptable to both parties and an agreement was reached on a security zone of 10km from the border, into which the aircraft of both countries would not enter. The Hungarians also banned the flights of agricultural aircraft without the special approval of the commander of the air force. Then, a permanent connection of air surveillance centres and data exchange was organised.

The position of the Croatian side was that the agreement did not apply to them, and for example, on 13 December, the commander of the Croatian unit from Virovitica informed the border unit in Barcz that an An-2 would be flying near the border. The command of the Hungarian border units informed the Yugoslav side that the Croats did not want to respect the government-to-government agreement on a no-fly zone of 10km because they did not recognise the government in Belgrade.

On 15 December, Hungarian air surveillance detected a low-speed target and an Mi-24 was sent to intercept it, but its crew failed to visually detect the aircraft, which was estimated to be from the Croatian side.[25]

Only one serious incident during months of fighting was fortunate for the Hungarian air defence, which maintained a high level of combat readiness all that time and vigilantly monitored the situation along the 623km border (measured along the curved 'green border' line) with the SFRJ from Slovenia, through Croatia and Serbia. Due to the war on the southern borders, Hungary made an effort to organise an effective system to protect its territory, which included air surveillance and missile battalions transferred from other parts of the country.

At that time, the Hungarians had three fighter regiments with about 40 MiG-21bis and about 10 MiG-21MFs and nine MiG-23MFs. The main burden of QRA tasks fell to the 59th Fighter Aviation Regiment (*59. Honi Vadászpülö Osztály*) from Kecskemét AB in the central part of Hungary, which was oriented towards Serbia and Eastern Slavonia. Also in a geographical position oriented towards Yugoslavia was the 31st Regiment from Taszár. As reinforcement for that unit, a number of MiG-21bis from the 47th Regiment was transferred from the base at Pápa in the southwest part of Hungary.

The air surveillance system organised in the 54th Radio-Technical Brigade (*54. Veszprém Rádiótechnikai Dandárparancsnokság*) concentrated a radar network to the south in the summer of 1991 in order to better cover the situation in the border zone. On the basis of an order from 23 and 26 August, radar units were moved to the southern borders on the Nagykanizsa–Szeged line. Radar sites were determined near the border line of Pórszombat, Szenta, Lakóca, Nagyharsány, Bácsalmás and Ásotthalom. Subsequently, some radars were moved, the one from Szenta to Berzencére and the radar from Bácsalmás to Madarasra.

At first, 412 people and 24 radars and 150 members of the land forces were engaged in the protection of the southern approaches of Hungary. The radars used were:

- SZT-68U (NATO codename 'Thin Shield', Soviet designation 36D6) 3D air surveillance radar that could detect a MiG-21-sized target at up to 136km and an altitude of 20km, with an accuracy of 250m by distance, 0.2° by angle or 0.4-1.5m by height.
- Kasta-2E (NATO codename 'Flat Face', Soviet designation Kasta-2E 39N6E) 3D radar that could detect a MiG-21-sized target at distance of 170km and an altitude of 6km.
- P-18 (NATO codename 'Spoon Rest') 2D radar that could detect a MiG-21-sized target at 245km and altitudes of 33km, with an accuracy of 1.8km by distance and 1.5° by angle.
- P-15 (NATO codename 'Flat Face A') 2D radar.
- PRV-16 (NATO codename 'Thin Skin B') height-finder radar that was integrated with 2D radars.
- P-37M (NATO codename 'Bar Lock') radars that could detect a MiG-21-sized target at up to 188km with theoretical accuracy of 500m by distance and 0.5° by angle. As both radars were 2D, i.e. only observation radars for measuring altitude, they were attached to the PRV-17 (NATO codename 'Odd Pair') radar post, which could determine the flight altitude of a MiG-21 with a precision of 1,000m and an angle of 2°.

According to Hungarian official data, a total of 119,967 flights were registered during the period August to December 1991, out of which 2,487 were identified as military and were carefully tracked. Violations of airspace were reported in 17 cases and involved 22 aircraft.[26]

A Hungarian MiG-21bis (version 75AP) taking-off from a grass runway at Pápa AB, in training carried out once a year. (Photo by Laszlo Javor)

In 1991 and 1992, MiG-21MFs from Kecskemét AB stood QRA to respond to airspace violations from the Yugoslav side. (Photo by Laszlo Javor)

APPENDICES

APPENDIX 1: YUGOSLAV, US AND BRITISH RANK EQUIVALENTS

Yugoslav Rank	**US Air Force Rank**	**Royal Air Force Rank**
	General of the Army (5-star)	Marshal of the Royal Air Force
general armije/General of the Army (4-star)	General (4-star)	Air Chief Marshal
general-pukovnik/Colonel-General (3-star)	Lieutenant General (3-star)	Air Marshal
general-potpukovnik/Lieutenant-General (2-star)	Major General (2-star)	Air Vice Marshal
general-major/Major-General (1-star)	Brigadier General (1-star)	Air Commodore
pukovnik/Colonel	Colonel	Group Captain
potpukovnik/Lieutenant-Colonel	Lieutenant Colonel	Wing Commander
major/Major	Major	Squadron Leader
kapetan 1. klase/Captain 1st Class		
kapetan/Captain	Captain	Flight Lieutenant
poručnik/1st Lieutenant	1st Lieutenant	Flying Officer
potporučnik/2nd Lieutenant	2nd Lieutenant	Pilot Officer
zastavnik 1. klase/Warrant Officer 1st Class	Chief Master Sergeant of the Air Force	Master Aircrew

APPENDIX 2: RV i PVO AIRCRAFT DESIGNATIONS

Factory Designation	**RV i PVO Designation**
L = lovacf (fighter aircraft)	
MiG-21PFM	L-14
MiG-21M/MF	L-15
MiG-21bis	L-17
MiG-21bis-K	L-17K with ARL-SM Lazur-M ground control intercept navigation system
MiG-29	L-18
NL = nastavni lovac (two-seat conversion trainer)	
MiG-21U	NL-12
MiG-21US	NL-14
MiG-21UM	NL-16
MiG-29UB	NL-18
I = izviđač (reconnaissance) M = modifikovani (modified)	
MiG-21R	L-14i
MiG-21MF with LOROP pod	L-15M
J = jurišni (attack)	
Kraguj	J-20
Jastreb J-1	J-21
Orao	J-22
IJ = izviđač jurišnik (reconnaissance-attack)	
Jastreb RJ-1	IJ-21
Orao	IJ-22
Orao with SLAR pod	INJ-22M
NJ = nastavni- jurišni (training-attack), INJ = izviđač-nastavni- jurišni (reconnaissance-training-attack)	
Jastreb TJ	NJ-21
Orao	INJ-22
Orao	NJ-22
N = nastavni (training)	
Galeb G-2A	N-60
Galeb G-2A of a newer series with enhanced avionics	N-60M ('M' is *modernizovani* – modernised)
Galeb G-4	N-62
Galeb G-4 target tug	N-62T ('T' is *tegljač* – tug)
Lasta	N-63
T = transportni (transport)	
Antonov An-26	T-70
V = veza (liaison)	
Utva-66	V-51
Utva-75	V-53 (the designation of this aircraft is unusual because by its real purpose it was strictly a trainer)
H = helicopter (helicopter)	
Mil Mi-8	HT-40 ('T' for transport aircraft)
Mi-8 for ELINT	HT-40E ('E' for *elektronski* – electronics)
SA 341H Gazelle	HO-42 ('O' for *opšti* – general purpose (utility))
SA 341H Gazelle search and rescue version	HS-42 ('S' for *spasilački* – rescue)
SA 341H Gazelle in reconnaissance version with project marking Hera	Hi-42 ('i' for *izviđač* – reconnaissance)
SA 341H Gazelle in attack version with project marking Gama	HN-42M ('N' is *naoružani* – armed, and 'M' is for Malytka anti-tank guided missile used by Gama version)
Kamov Ka-25PL	HP-43 ('P' is *protivpodmornički* – anti-submarine)
Mil Mi-14PL	HP-44
SA 342L Gazelle	HO-45 (most frequently the simplified generic marking H-45 is used in documents)
SA 342L Gazelle in attack version Gama	HN-45M
Kamov Ka-28	HP-46

BIBLIOGRAPHY

Anon., *Ratni album 109. brigade HV Vinkovci* (Vinkovci: Slavonska naklada Privlačica, Vinkovci, 1992)

Bošković, Rajica, *Nebo na dlanu* (Beograd: self-published, 2017)

Božić, Aleksandar & Damir Goršeta, *153. velikogorička brigada HV* (Zagreb: Turopoljski glasnik d.o.o. and the Udruga pripadnika 153. brigade HV, 2022)

Brigović, Ivan & Ivan Radoš, *101. brigada HV-a* (Zagreb: UHBDR 101. brigade Susedgrad, HMDCDR, 2013)

Cišper, Zlatko, *Zapovjedništvo Zbora narodne garde Republike Hrvatske, 1991. Godine* (Zagreb: Branitelji Hrvatske, 2011)

Davor, Marijan, *Bitka za Vukovar 1991* (Zagreb-Slavonski Brod: Hrvatski institut za povijest, Podružnica za povijest Slavonije, Srijema i Baranje, 2004)

Davor Marijan, *Graničari – Prilog za ratni put 108. brigade Zbora narode garde RH* (Slavonski Brod: Hrvatski institut za povijest, Podružnica za povijest Slavonije, Srijema i Baranje, 2006)

Dimitrijević, Bojan B., *Kurjaci sa Ušća* (Beograd: ISI, 2004)

Ivanić, Stjepan, *Da se ne zaboravi, 105. brigada HV-a u Domovinskom ratu 1991.-1992.*(Bjelovar: Udruga 105. brigade HV-a, 2006)

Lučić, Josip (ed.), *Prva gardijska brigada Hrvatske vojske Tigrovi* (Zagreb: Znanje, 2015)

Kadijević, Veljko, *Protiv udar* (Beograd: IP Filip Višnjić, 2010)

Mihanović, Ivan, 'Borbe za vojarne i oružje u Osijeku 1991', *Polemos* 19, 2016

Najman, Dujić, Posilović, *Bloklade i osvajanje vojarni i vojnih objekata JNA u Hrvatskoj* (Zagreb: Udruga dragovoljaca Narodne zaštite Domovinskog rata, 2004)

Najman, Dujić, Posilović, *Bloklade i osvajanje vojarni i vojnih objekata JNA u Hrvatskoj – grad Zagreb* (Zagreb: Udruga dragovoljaca Narodne zaštite Domovinskog rata, 2005)

Radić, Aleksandar, *The Yugoslav Air Force in the Battles for Slovenia, Croatia and Bosnia and Herzegovina, 1991–1992 Volume 1* (Warwick: Helion & Company, 2020)

Šlezak, Mladen, *Prva postrojba protuzračne obrane grada Zagreba* (Zagreb: privately published, 2017)

Stipčić, Rudi, *Napokon smo krenuli...*(Zagreb: Sveučilišna tiskara, 1996)

Stipčić, Rudi, *Zagrebački korpus Zbora narodne garde, 3. Operativna zona Zagreb* (Sisak: Karmen komunikacije, 2018)

Szabó, Pál József, *Radarokkal a lopakodók ellen (A magyar katonai légtérellenörzö és radarrendszer története 1917-2014)* (Budapest: Zrínyi Kiadó, 2014)

Vidaković, Melia & Davorin Strišković, *Donji Miholjac u Domovinskom ratu* (Donji Miholjac: Pauk Cerna, 2007)

Virc, Zlatko, *109. brigada na vratima Hrvatske (1991.-1992.)* (Vinkovci: Udruga dragovoljaca i veterana domovinskog rata)

Željko, Karaula, 'Osvajanje vojarne JNA "Božidar Adžija" in Bejlovar 1991' (Zagreb: *Časopis za suvremenu povijest*, Vol 39 No 1, 2007)

Zvonimir, Lulić and Janko, Povše, *Protuzračna obrana Kvarnera, Like i Istre u Domovinskom ratu 1991.-1996.* (Zagreb: self-published, 2016)

Documentation

Documents from the Military Archive, Belgrade, Aeronautical Museum in Surčin, and Command of the JRV i PVO.

ENDNOTES

Chapter 1

1 Zvonimir, Lulić and Janko, Povše, *Protuzračna obrana Kvarnera, Like i Istre u Domovinskom ratu 1991.-1996.* (Zagreb: self-published, 2016).

2 Using the example of the Air Force Academy (*Vazduhoplovna vojna akademija*, VVA) in 1991: 102 pilots, 26 air technical and other officers, 154 NCOs, 33 VVA cadets, 32 students of the Air Military Gymnasium and 30 civilians left its command and four regiments. Of that number, 126 people deserted, including 29 officers, 28 NCOs and eight cadets. A total of 61 soldiers escaped from barracks (Analysis of combat training, education and combat readiness in the VVA in 1991).

3 Analiza borbene obuke i vaspitanja i borbene gotovosti u VVA 1991. document from Command of RV i PVO.

4 Radić, Aleksandar, *The Yugoslav Air Force in the Battles for Slovenia, Croatia and Bosnia and Herzegovina, 1991–1992, Volume 1* (Warwick: Helion & Co, 2020), pp.71, 74.

5 Veljko Kadijević (1925–2014) was the Federal Secretary for National Defence (equivalent to the Minister of Defence) from 15 May 1988 to 8 January 1992 and at the same time the chief of the ŠVK during the war. He was born in 1925 in Dalmatia in an ethnically mixed family – his father was a Serb and mother a Croat. He grew up in a leftist environment. Kadijević's father was a member of the International Brigade in the Spanish Civil War, where he died in 1936. In 1943, at the age of 18, Kadijević became a partisan guerrilla and a member of the Communist Party. After the war, he remained in military service and reached the rank of general with one star in 1966; an unusual precedent in the JNA is the fact that he was a general for more than 25 years. Ironically, while completing his highest military education at the US Army Command and Staff College, during the wars in Yugoslavia, he became an ideological hardliner and sought the support of the Russian Federation, while developing a growing distance from Western influence. After retirement from the military, Kadijević also retired from public life and moved to Moscow in 2001, where he died in 2014 as a Russian citizen.

6 Kadijević, Veljko, *Protiv udar* (Beograd: IP Filip Višnjić, 2010).

7 The Croatian Army (*Hrvatska vojska*, HV) was organised by the presidential act on military-territorial defence from 30 September 1991, at the beginning of autumn in accordance with the geographical characteristics of the battlefield. Six commands of operative zones (*operativna zona*, OZ) were formed, which had zones of responsibility from the east to west; the 1st OZ Osijek (Eastern Slavonija), 2nd OZ Bjelovar (Western Slavonija), 3rd OZ Zagreb (Banija and Pokuplje), 4th OZ Karlovac (Karlovac and the Kordun region), 5th OZ Rijeka (Lika region), and the 6th OZ Split (Dalmatia). Two sub-commands were also established for the areas of Zadar (northern Dalmacija) and Dubrovnik (southern Dalmacija).

8 Lučić , Josip (ed.), *Prva gardijska brigada Hrvatske vojske Tigrovi* (Zagreb: Znanje, 2015), pp.86, 130.

9 Zlatko, Cišper, *Zapovjedništvo Zbora narodne garde Republike Hrvatske, 1991. Godine* (Zagreb: Branitelji Hrvatske, 2011), p.344.

10 Analiza borbene obuke i vaspitanja i borbene gotovosti u VVA 1991. document from Command of RV i PVO.

ABOUT THE AUTHOR

Aleksandar Radić is a Serbian military analyst and author. His primary focus is on the security topics of the western Balkans, the history of the armed forces and military technology in that region in the twentieth century, and the conflicts that followed the break-up of Yugoslavia between 1991 and 2001. He has authored a dozen books and hundreds of magazine articles published in the specialist press. Radić also frequently appears as military commentator for major TV stations in Serbia, Montenegro, Bosnia and Herzegovina, and the Republic of Northern Macedonia.

down in 1991. He died in 2013 from cancer. His pair leader Lovrić died in an accident with a MiG-21bis in 1993. Rajica Bošković, *Nebo na dlanu* (Beograd, autorsko izdanje, 2017), pp.367–371, 434–438.

4 Rudi Stipčić, *Zagrebački korpus Zbora narodne garde, 3. Operativna zona Zagreb* (Sisak: Karmen komunikacije, 2018), p.14.

Chapter 4

1 Radić, pp.49–50.

2 According to the order from the commander of the RV i PVO, dated 6 October, the existing 111th Air Brigade was disbanded. Its 679th Squadron with Antonov An-26 aircraft, which was then stationed at Batajnica air base, was subordinated to the local 138th Brigade. The 713th Squadron was disbanded. From the remaining units, the 111th Helicopter Regiment was formed by this order, with the 711th Squadron and the 780th Squadron stationed at Zalužani. The order had to be executed by 12 October. The ceremonial formation of the new regiment took place on October.

3 In August, changes were ordered in the Command of the RV i PVO from 'A' to 'B' classification for the 474th Air Base, but the war intervened in those plans. Based on the order issued on 6 October, the 474th Air Base retained its 'A' classification, with command and the majority of subordinated units in Banja Luka base. The 81st Company for aviation support remained at Zalužani airfield, and the 82nd Company was located at Urije airfield near Prijedor, intended only for wartime development. Additional changes were implemented by the order issued on 8 November, which replaced the 81st Squadron with the formation of the 51st Battalion in Zalužani to support the 111th Regiment. It was planned that, in the event of war, the 43rd Company would be formed at Urije airfield, but since the wartime period was not declared, the unit was not mobilised.

4 *1 Gardijska brigada Hrvatske vojske Tigrovi* (Zagreb: Znanje, 2015), pp.180–181.

5 Rudi Stipčić: *Napokon smo krenuli...* (Zagreb: Sveučilišna tiskara, 1996), pp.23, 108. http://novska.hr/hr/on-line-vijesti/komemorativni-skup-u-sjecanje-na-zrtve-4-listopada-1991-godine,5729.html, accessed 12.01.2020.

6 Vojna povijest 86, p.17.

Chapter 5

1 A mechanised brigade in the JNA had two mechanised and two tank battalions with 83 T-55 or T-72M/M-84 MBTs and 61 M-60P/PB APCs or M-80/M-80A IFVs. Artillery support for the brigades included a battalion each with two batteries of six 2S1 Gvozdika self-propelled howitzers and one battery with six M-63 Plamen MRLs. The air defence element was a battalion with two batteries of ZSU-57/2 or M53/59 AA guns each and a battery of six 9P31M Strela-1M SAM launchers. The anti-armoured battalion had two batteries, each with six M36 or SU-100 tank destroyers and a battery of 9P133 or M-83 launchers.

2 A motorised brigade in the JNA had three motorised battalions, infantry units with soft-skinned all-terrain vehicles, one armoured battalion with T-55 or T-34 tanks, a howitzer artillery battalion with 105mm (M2A1 or M56) or 122mm (D30 or M38) howitzers, a mixed anti-tank artillery battalion (two batteries M36 90mm self-propelled guns or towed T-12 100mm guns and one battery of 9K11 anti-tank guided missiles), a light artillery air defence battalion (M55 20/3 or M53/59 30/2 AA guns), an engineer battalion, a logistic battalion and directly subordinated units of military police, communication, and CBRN defence, etc.

3 The only active division in the structure of the JNA in 1991 was the manoeuvring structure with three 'proletarian guard mechanised brigades' with numerical markings in a sequence, the 1st from Belgrade garrison, 2nd from Valjevo and 3rd from Požarevac. The structure of the division included the 1st Guard Mixed Artillery Regiment from Kragujevac, 1st Guard Mixed Anti-Armour Artillery Regiment from Belgrade and 1st Air Defence Regiment from Belgrade.

4 Unit directly subordinated to the SSNO (*Savezni sekretarijat za narodnu odbranu*, Federal Secretariat for National Defence, the SFRJ equivalent to the Ministry of Defence, 1971–1992), stationed in the Belgrade garrison. It consisted of the Protection Battalion, two motorised battalions, two military police battalions, armoured battalion, air defence battalion and armoured-mechanised battalion. During the war, the unit had around 3,500 people.

5 Ivan Mihanović, *Borbe za vojarne i oružje u Osijeku 1991*, Polemos 19, 2016.

6 Najman, Dujić, Posilović, pp.322–324; Melia Vidaković i Davorin Strišković, *Donji Miholjac u Domovinskom ratu* (Donji Miholjac: Pauk Cerna, 2007), pp.6–7, 14, 51.

7 The pilot was armed with a 7.65mm M84 machine pistol, a licence copy of the Czechoslovakian Vz. 61, manufactured by Crvena Zastava. In was known in the JNA by its original name Škorpion (Scorpion).

8 Ranđelović saw the Croats open fire on a pair of MiG-21 from the 126th Squadron with one rocket, the planes struck and left. Croatian sources say that, according to their assessment, one MiG-21 was shot down. The second one hit the courtyard of a company called Analit and the parking lot of the Borik hotel. Besides material damage, there were no casualties. Vidaković, Strišković, p.39.

9 Front, 1992, Noga puna gvožđa.

10 Bojan B. Dimitrijević, *Kurjaci sa Ušća* (Beograd: ISI, 2004), p.42.

11 Davor Marijan, *Bitka za Vukovar 1991* (Zagreb-Slavonski Brod: Hrvatski institut za povijest, Podružnica za povijest Slavonije, Srijema i Baranje, 2004).

12 Zlatko Virc, *109. brigada na vratima Hrvatske (1991.-1992.)* (Vinkovci: Udruga dragovoljaca i veterana domovinskog rata), pp.127–128, 172, 179–182.

13 Croatian sources confirm that there was a triple 20mm M55A4 in Durgutovici, mounted on a FAP truck. *Ratni album 109. brigade HV Vinkovci* (Vinkovci: Slavonska naklada Privlačica, Vinkovci), p.99.

14 Davor Marijan, Bitka za Vukovar 1991. *Scrinia Slavonica* 2 (2002), pp.367–402.

15 Švarm, Skrozza, Vasić, Vukovarska apokalipsa, Vreme news magazin, 25 October 2011. Mirčetić (1938–2015) was a representative of the hard-line Yugoslav current that firmly held the Command of the RV i PVO during the war in 1991. He studied at the Air Force Academy in 1957–1960 in the XIII class on the Aero-3 and 522 piston trainer. For the first eight years of his career, he was an instructor on the TV-2 (US Navy designation for T-33A) and F-86E Sabre. After retraining for the MiG-21, he quickly rose through the ranks. From 1981 to 1985, he was the deputy commander of the 15th Air Defence Division, a unit responsible for the defence of the western part of the country, which included the Bihać-based 117th Brigade with MiG-21 and air surveillance and air defence missile units. He was the division commander in 1985/1986 and when V Corps of the RV i PVO was formed, he was the Chief of Staff of that formation, and from 1987 to 1990, its commander. From 1990 to the beginning of 1992, he was Chief of Staff Command of the RV i PVO and for a short time in January and February 1992 acting CO.

16 Stjepan Ivanić, *Da se ne zaboravi, 105. brigada HV-a u Domovinskom ratu 1991.-1992.* (Bjelovar: Udruga 105. brigade HV-a, 2006), p.123.

17 Davor Marijan, Bjelovar i Bjelovarsko-Bilogorska županija u Domovinskom ratu, Radovi Zavoda za znanstvenoistraživački i umjetnički rad u Bjelovaru, 8/2014, p.34.

18 Željo Rukavina, I fired on a MiG, and only in the evening I found out I shot it down, 24. sata, 29.11.2018.

19 Ustašas were Croatian Nazis from the Second World War. The term was used by the Serbians as a slur for all the Croat forces in 1991.

20 In 1992, Halilović became the Chief of Staff of the Army of Bosnia-Herzegovina. In the autumn of 1993, he commanded over actions against the Croatian forces in Herzegovina.

21 Chetniks were Serbian quislings from the Second World War and the term was used as a slur by Croats.

22 Davor Marijan: *Graničari – Prilog za ratni put 108. brigade Zbora narode garde RH* (Slavonski Brod: Hrvatski institut za povijest, Podružnica za povijest Slavonije, Srijema i Baranje, 2006), p.73.

23 Davor Marijan: *Graničari – Prilog za ratni put 108. brigade Zbora narode garde RH* (Slavonski Brod: Hrvatski institut za povijest, Podružnica za povijest Slavonije, Srijema i Baranje, 2006), p.73.

24 Marijan, p.104.

25 Documents of RV i PVO on Yugoslav-Hungarian relations during 1991, archive of RV i PVO.

26 Szabó Pál József, *Radarokkal a lopakodók ellen (A magyar katonai légtérellenörzö és radarrendszer története 1917-2014)* (Budapest: Zrínyi Kiadó, 2014).

Chapter 2

1 Bošković, pp.440–442; Željko Karaula: Osvajanje vojarne JNA "Božidar Adžija" in Bejlovar 1991 (Zagreb: *Časopis za suvremenu povijest*, Vol 39 No 1, 2007).

2 Rajica Bošković, *Nebo na dlanu* (Beograd: autorsko izdanje, 2017), pp.367–371, 434–438.

3 Unit of brigade level, which according to formation determined on 6 September 1991, was supposed to have a Command, a company for air technical and technical maintenance, a company for air technical and technical supply, an automobile company, an infantry company, an engineer company, signal company, quartermaster company, military police platoon (in wartime, a company), a platoon for support to aviation (in wartime, a company), firefighting platoon, Nuclear Biological and Chemical Defence platoon, airfield OC and meteorological station (in wartime), photo section, ambulance (in wartime, a medical platoon), military construction section (in wartime, a construction platoon), the service of thermo-energy (only in peacetime), the 151st Air Defence Light Artillery and Missile Battalion and the 96th Company for support too.

4 The order for the 265th Mechanised Brigade and the 73rd Mechansied Brigade, from XXXII Corps, was to break through from Bjelovar towards a place called Grubišno Polje and continue towards Daruvar in West Slavonia. These units surrendered a couple of days after the order for the breakout was signed.

5 The introduction of units from Slovenia into combat was abandoned. According to the basic agreement between the Federal authorities and Slovenia, the personnel were evacuated by sea, and the weapons were formally left in the temporary custody of the Slovenian TO. The Slovenians used the weapons to replenish the Slovenian armed forces.

6 Najman, Dujić, Posilović, *grad Zagreb*, p.35.

7 Mladen Šlezak, *Prva postrojba protuzračne obrane grada Zagreba* (Zagreb: privatno izdanje, 2017), p.23.

8 Najman, Dujić, Posilović, grad Zagreb, pp.140–143.

9 Minutes of examination of witnesses Colonel Marijant Vratović pred istražiteljom službe za ratne zločine policije u Puli, 4 October 2017, note.

10 Šlezak, pp.27–32.

11 Lučić , *Prva gardijska brigada Hrvatske vojske Tigrovi* (Zagreb: Znanje, 2015), p.154.

12 Renata Rašović, Prvi helikopter zvan Stara frajla branio je hrvatsko nebo punih deset godina, Večernji list, 23 September 2016. Note, in Lučko, Mi-8 number 12271 was repainted in a camouflage scheme and was given Croatian markings, the designation H-101 and the nickname *Stara frajla*. In the fall of 1991, it was an extremely important aircraft for the Croatian forces, but it was almost destroyed by friendly fire on 4 November over the Zagreb neighbourhood of Šestine when heavy fire was opened from automatic rifles and the 'eight' was damaged.

13 Najman, Dujić, Posilović, grad Zagreb, pp.120–121.

14 Bošković, p.440, Prošlo je 30 godina: Vlado and Neven prvi su poginuli gorički branitelji, stradali u raketiranju zrakoplova JNA na Sajmištu | VG danas.

15 Dražen Najman, Ivan Posilović and Marija Dijuć, p.34.

16 State Attorney's Office of the Republic of Croatia (dorh.hr) County State Attorney's Office in Zagreb Indictment brought against six defendants for attempted murder of representatives of the highest state bodies and war crimes against the civilian population.

17 Večernje Novosti, General Ljubomir Bajić on the rocketing of Banski dvor 15.12.2017.

18 HRABRI SINOVI DOMOVINE: VARAŽDINSKE 'RODE' (2/4) | Domoljubni portal CM | U vihoru rata (crnemambe.hr)

19 Prva velikogorička topnička bojna: They defied the enemy with only four mortars and one rifle for several soldiers! | VG danas.

20 Ivan Brigović and Ivan Radoš, *101. brigada HV-a* (Zagreb: UHBDR 101. brigade Susedgrad, HMDCDR, 2013) p.54; *153. velikogorička brigada HV* (Zagreb: Turopoljski glasnik d.o.o. and the Udruga pripadnika 153. brigade HV, 2022), pp.84–86.

21 Šlezak, pp.59–60.

22 The OSCE study on liquid rocket fuel states that 'contact with nitric acid or inhalation of nitric gases will result in severe cauterization of skin, mucous membranes, the respiratory system (pulmonary oedema) and eyes'. Nitric acid makes no less than 73 percent of the mix. Other ingredients are also very dangerous. Nitrogen Tetraoxide, 17.5–22.5 percent of the mix, according to the OSCE 'inhalation of nitric gases will result in lungs evolving slowly and their becoming progressively inflamed. It is dangerous for the skin mucous membranes, the respiratory system (pulmonary oedema) and eyes'. Rocket fuel contains a mixture of 50–52 percent technical triethylamine with a small quantity of diethylamide and 48–50 percent of the mixture of technical isomer xylidines and presents as a yellow to dark-brown mobile oily liquid with odor typical of fatty amines. Contact with triethylamine mainly results in local effects. Eye contact causes severe burns. Clothing wet with triethylamine will cause skin burns. Carcinogenic (skin), temporary blue hazy vision, vapours irritate nose, throat, lung, causing coughing, choking and difficult breathing. Isomers are poisonous, creating headache and dizziness and are carcinogenic. OESC document *Liquid Rocket Fuel in the OSCE Area: Overview of Disposal Aspects* (Vienna: OSCE, 2008), pp.6–7.

23 portal Croatian Institute of Public Health – Department for ToxicologyKNJIGA (hzt.hr)

24 Najman, Dujić and Posilović, book 2, pp.184–185.

25 Najman, Dujić and Posilović, book 2, pp.211–217.

26 27. obljetnica 55. LAD PZO Sisak – Sisak.info portal.

27 Rajica Bošković, *Nebo na dlanu* (Beograd, author`s edition, 2017), pp.438–439, Najman, Dujić, Posilović, city of Zagreb, pp.208–209; Stipčić, p.87; Marijan Celjak (uhbhep.hr); OBLJETNICE: Sjećanje na Marijana Celjaka Bobana, istinskog heroja obrane Siska (maxportal.hr), Boris Gregurić, Špareti iz Siska, Hrvatski vojnik, 7 August 2020. note – In 1993, the 57th Battalion grew into the 57th Brigade, which bore the name Marijan Celjak.

28 Lieutenant Colonel Radoljub Gajić, a famous Yugoslav MiG pilot was killed in an Utva-66. He was going out of an active unit and received a transfer to the air traffic control in Banja Luka. Behind him was the career of a pilot who had made many Cold War-era flights near the borders of neighbouring countries with recon versions of MiGs. In one flight in a MiG-21MF equipped with a LORAP (Long Range Aerial Panoramic Photographic) system, accompanied by a MiG-21R with ELINT, he photographed the whole of Albania. He flew from Golubovci to the Gulf of Otranto and back, and returned to his starting base. Gajić wanted to celebrate his new job and officers from Bihać say that he and his colleagues drank alcoholic beverages. During the take-off, Gajić and Selak 'fought' for the pilot's stick and this led to the accident. After long treatment in Belgrade, Selak returned to the unit. He later became known to the public in the West Balkans after flying from Serbia to Croatia with a MiG-21bis on 15 May 1992. He flew combat missions in the Croatian Air Force during the war. Now Colonel Ret is a frequent guest in the Croatian media due to his sober stance on issues related to aviation.

Chapter 3

1 The RV i PVO's radar systems of the S-600 family, manufactured by the British company Marconi, were procured in 1971. The modular system had independent antennas for surveillance radar and altitude radar, transmitter-receiver cabins, and operational cabins. The first generation, acquired in 1971, consisted of the analogue Brandy system. Subsequently, from 1974, digital Bridge systems were procured, and equipped with the OK Furnus, which simultaneously served as an element of the AS-74 command and information system. At the Ljubljanski Vrh and Plješevica sites, there were Bridge systems with the S-1020 stationary antenna for surveillance radar in the D-band, S-654M (Master), and S-654S (Slave) transmitter-receiver cabins, S-1017 height-finder antenna in the G/H-band with S-613 transmitter-receiver cabin, S-5014B OK with two Locus 16 computers (Till and Dol), and the AS-74 system also with two Locus 16 computers. The difference between OK and AS-74 was in the software, as the former device supported the operation of a fourth-level radar station, while the command and information system operated at the battalion level as AS-75. Simultaneously, it served as the basis for the command post of the 350th Air Defence Missile Regiment in Vrhnika barracks, part of the 91st Air Surveillance Battalion, and the command post of the 117th Aviation Brigade in Bihać air base, part of the 51st Air Surveillance Battalion.

2 In the SFRJ, the air traffic control system was integrating civilian and military operations, but the leading position in every of air traffic centre was held by an officer of the RV i PVO.

3 After returning to his unit, Mandić continued to fly MiG-21s, although he had ejected twice – in an accident in 1989 and when shot

2 sts, long sc in next st 4 rows below; rep from * across to last 3 sts, sc in last 3 sts, changing to MC in last st, turn—46 (49, 52) sc.

Rows 15 – 34 (34, 38): Repeat Rows 11 – 14.

Row 35 (35, 39): Using MC, work even.

Shape Armhole

Row 36 (36, 40): Slip st across first 4 sts; ch 1, sc in same space and in each st across to last 3 sts, turn; leave remaining sts unworked—40 (43, 46) sc remain.

Next Row: Sc2tog across first 2 sts, sc in each st across to last 2 sts, sc2tog, changing to A in last st, turn—38 (41, 44) sc.

Next Row: Sc2tog, work in pattern across to last 2 sts, sc2tog, changing to MC in last st, turn—36 (39, 42) sc.

Next Row: S2tog, sc in each st across to last 2 sts, sc2tog, turn—34 (37, 40) sc.

Work even in pattern until armhole measures 4 1/2" from beginning of shaping. Fasten off.

FRONT (make 2, reversing shaping)

Using A, chain 22 (25, 28).

Row 1: Sc in second ch from hook and in each ch across, turn—21 (24, 27) sc.

Rows 2 - 13: Work as for Back.

Row 14: Using A, ch 1, sc in first st, long sc in next st 4 rows below, * sc in each of next 2 sts, long sc in next st 4 rows below; rep from * across to last 2 sts, sc in last 2 sts, changing to MC in last st, turn.

Work as for Back, in pattern as established, to beginning of armhole shaping—21 (24, 27) sc; Row 35 (35, 39 completed).

Shape Armhole

Row 36 (36, 40): At armhole edge, slip st across first 4 sts; ch 1, sc in same space and in each st across, turn—18 (21, 24) sc remain.

Next Row: Sc in each st across to last 2 sts, sc2tog, changing to A in last st, turn—17 (20, 23) sc remain.

Next Row: Sc2tog, work in pattern across, changing to MC in last st, turn—16 (19, 22) sc remain.

Next Row: Sc in each st across to last 2 sts, sc2tog, turn—15 (18, 21) sc.

Work even in pattern until armhole measures 2 1/2" from beginning of shaping. Fasten off, turn.

Shape Neck

Row 51 (51, 55): Continuing in pattern as established, at neck edge, skip 5 (7, 9) sts, join MC with a slip st in next st; ch 1, sc in same space and in each st across, turn—10 (11, 12) sc.

Row 52 (52, 56): Work across to last 2 sts, sc2tog, turn—9 (10, 11) sc.

Row 53 (53, 57): Sc2tog, sc in each st across, changing to A while finishing last st, turn—8 (9, 10) sc.

Row 54 (54, 58): Work across to last 2 sts, sc2tog, changing to MC in last st, turn—7 (8, 9) sc.

Work even until armhole measures 4 1/2" from beginning of shaping.

Fasten off.

SLEEVES (make 2)

Using A, chain 30 (33, 36).

Row 1: Sc in second ch from hook and in each ch across, turn—29 (32, 35) sc.

Rows 2 - 13: Work as for Back.

Row 14: Ch 1, sc in first st, long sc in next st 4 rows below, * sc in next 2 sts, long sc in next st 4 rows below; rep from * across, changing to MC in last st, turn.

Rows 15 – 38 (38, 42):
Repeat Rows 11 – 14.

Shape Cap
Row 39 (39, 43): Continuing in Pattern, slip st across first 4 sts; ch 1, sc in same space and in each st across to last 3 sts, turn; leave remaining sts unworked—23 (26, 29) sts remain.
Row 40 (40, 44): Sc2tog, sc in each st across to last 2 sts, sc2tog, changing to A in last st, turn—21 (24, 27) sts remain.
Work even for 2 rows.
Decrease Row: Sc2tog, sc in each st to last 2 sts, sc2tog, turn—19 (22, 25) sts remain.
Work even for 3 rows.
Work Decrease Row—17 (20, 23) sts remain.
Work even for 2 rows.
Work Decrease Row, this row, then every other row 5 times—5 (8, 11) sts remain.
Using A, work even for 0 (0, 3) rows.
Fasten off.

HOOD
Using A, chain 67 (70, 73).
Row 1: Sc in second ch from hook and in each ch across, turn—66 (69, 72) sc.
Rows 2 – 13: Work as for Back.
Row 14: Begin pattern as for Sleeve.
Continue in pattern established [repeat Rows 11 – 14] 8 (9, 10) times, and AT THE SAME TIME, dec 1 st each side every 3 (3, 4) rows 7 times, every other row 4 times, then every row 3 times—38 (41, 44) sts remain.

Shape Back of Hood
Next Row: Slip st across first 10 sts, work as established to last 10 sts, turn, leaving remaining sts unworked—18 (21, 21) sts remain.
Work even as established for 22 (26, 30) rows for Back of Hood.
Fasten off.

FINISHING
Using yarn needle, weave in all ends.
Sew shoulder seams. Sew in Sleeves; sew side and Sleeve seams. Sew Back of Hood to sides of Hood.

Jacket Edging
With RS facing, join A with a slip st to lower edge of right Front; ch 1, sc in end of each row to upper edge of right Front, work 3 sc in last row. Fasten off.

With RS facing, join A to upper edge of left Front; ch 1, work 3 sc in first row, sc in end of each row to lower edge of left Front. Fasten off.

Using sewing thread and needle, sew zipper in place.
Attach Hood to neckline; weave in ends.

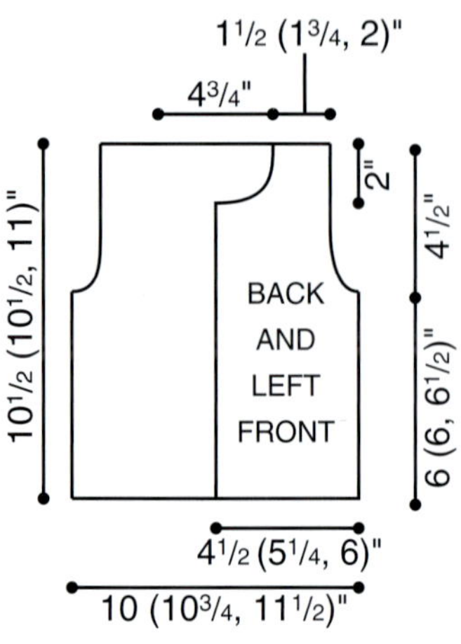

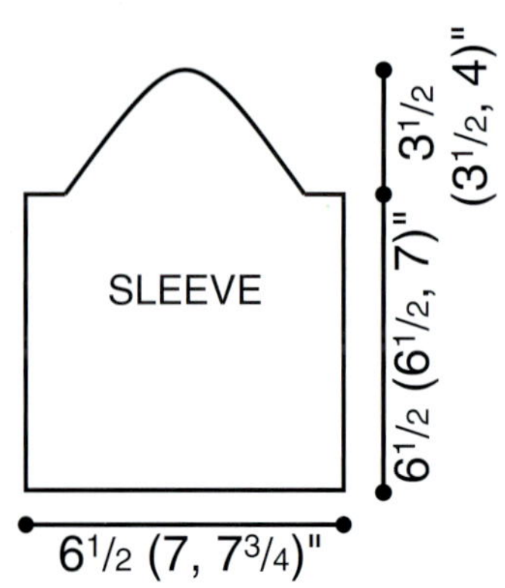

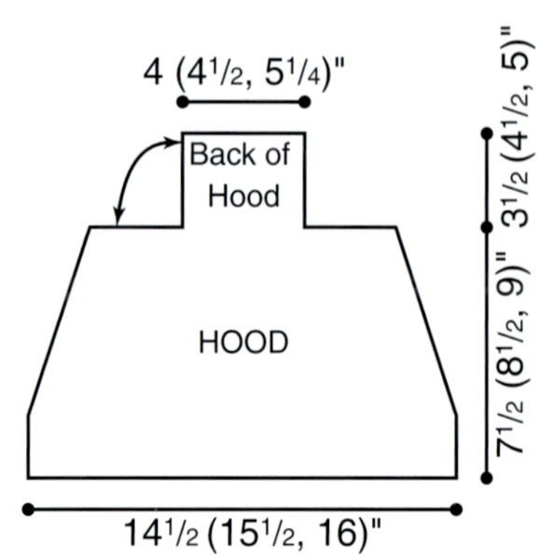